What others are saying about—
My Life as a Sales Engineer

"I believe you will find Jerry's book compelling; it is rare that you will find a sales professional able to articulate a 'philosophy' of the noble profession of sales. In fact, the life lessons illustrated in this book reinforce the value of being genuine, sincere, and above all, having the humility to not take yourself too seriously! A great read!"

Douglas Polk, Vice President of Sales, Service and Marketing, VAM USA

"Jerry's book is a lesson in true perseverance—a key attribute for any successful technical sales person."

Jim Burtner, P.E.—Former VP North America Sales and Operations and VP Worldwide Marketing and Technology, Baker Oil Tools Division, Baker Hughes, Inc.

"The first time we met Jerry Rubli, we were pleased that a person with his education and previous sales experience would respond to our ad in the newspaper and later become a part of Choctaw Sales. He was eager to learn the packaging industry but because he'd been recently laid off from a long-term salaried position and had the responsibility of a family, he was concerned about his portion of the funds. When we told him he must have a 'Choctaw Heart' (my term for commissions) he was committed to learn all the possible places our service could be used.

"My husband Pat was the perfect bridge for him, having been involved in the oil industry at a young age, and Jerry was receptive to learning a number of sales concepts and principles from him. Pat has been called to a higher project with the Lord and I'm sure he'd be pleased that Jerry is sharing these thoughts with others."

Anne Curtin, President, Choctaw Sales

"This book is a must read! Whether you are just starting out or are an experienced technical sales professional, Jerry's book leads you through all the passageways to a rewarding career with insightful analogies, real life scenarios and 'tricks of the trade' when the going gets tough..."

Ben Matthews, Former Vice President,
Coil Tubing Division, Superior Energy Services

"Although the industry I am in is not close to Jerry's, many of his experiences, tips for selling and his approach to technical sales mirrors what I also have seen in my career. This book is a valuable tool for any technical salesperson whether he or she contemplates going into this profession or the veteran who wants to feel like they are not alone in facing the same challenges Jerry did. A great resource!"

Jon Symko, General Sales Manager,
Hunton Trane Services

"Great book. It's a road map for all who have walked the walk and an instruction manual for those beginning the journey. It should be mandatory reading for all who want to take the trip. For those of us who have been involved in technical sales, we can relate our own experiences to every detail Jerry describes. Brilliantly done."

John Harvey, Vice President, Hamilton Metals

"I've known Jerry for over thirty years and he has always looked for ways to contribute to the benefit of others. By sharing his experiences and professional approach to sales he has written a must read for those entering such a career as well as an interesting look back for the old-timers. I wish I had such a book thirty-three years ago!"

Bob Gibbens, Salesman, Entrepreneur, Investor,
Quality Rental Tools, United Machine Works

"Jerry's story of his industrial sales success is based on principles that can be applied to any selling situation. Well written, impactful, informative; this is a treasure trove of useful ideas valuable to anyone seeking to improve sales results."

Mel Amick, Founder, MAC,
Executive Coach and Leadership Training Facilitator

"I've enjoyed reading this book—it is right on the mark. If it had been available twenty-five years ago my learning curve in selling technical products would have been much faster".

Rickey Seagraves, Partner, International Lift Systems

My Life as a Sales Engineer

My Life as a Sales Engineer

The How-To Book of Technical Sales

Jerry Rubli, PE

Whitecaps Media
Houston

Whitecaps Media
Houston, Texas
www.whitecapsmedia.com

My Life as a Sales Engineer: The How-To Book of Technical Sales
© 2008 by Jerry Rubli

ISBN 978-0-9758577-6-2

Designed by Kit Sublett

Printed in the United States of America

The author welcomes your comments and inquires and can be reached by email at jrubli@earthlink.net

Dedication

To my wife Donna,
who has always encouraged me to do my best.

Acknowledgements

I am indebted to so many for all their help in shaping my life and my career:

—to the Good Lord, who inspired me to write this book.

—to my parents, Henry and Lois Rubli. Their hard work, Christian example and dedication to their family encouraged me, even as a child, to be industrious.

—to my wife, Donna, and our children and their families: Jason and Ashley Rubli, Olivier and Angie Simottel, and Kate Rubli. They made me have a reason for doing my best, even when things looked hopeless.

—to all my business associates and customers along the way. Without interaction with you, this book would not have been possible.

Contents

Introduction 9

1 My First Sales Engineering Assignment 13

First Selling Experiences 15

Training 17

The Product Offering 24

Being Unique 26

Product Management 27

Summary 30

2 Another Opportunity 33

Oilfield Pipe 33

National Account Management 35

New Product Introduction 37

Summary 41

3 Long-Term Consulting 43

Qualification Testing 44

Expert Witnessing 49

Getting Paid 51

Summary 55

4 Manufacturer's Representative 57

First Big Sale 60

More Projects 61

Sales Techniques 65

Engineering and Construction Companies 68

Being Organized Pays Off 72

Summary 75

5 Short-Term Consulting 77

Pulsation Dampeners 78

High Pressure Flanges 79

Plug Valves 80

Stereolithography 83

Summary 85

6 A New Material for an Old Industry 87

All About Titanium 88

Titanium Tubing 90

Titanium Tapered Stress Joints 92

Titanium Drill Pipe 96

Other Applications 100

Summary 100

7 Changing Jobs Again 103

Promotional Tools 104

Being Bold 107

Marketing to Small Firms 110

Computer Use 112

Presentations 114

Being Unique 117

Summary 120

8 Other Things I've Learned 123

The Sales Engineer's Role 123

Selling Techniques 124

Entertainment 128

When A Mistake is Made 131

Negotiating 134

When You Lose a Sale 135

9 Sales Engineering: A Wonderful Profession . . . 137

Topical Index 141

Introduction

*Choose a job you love and you will never have to work a
day in your life.*

—Confucius

It happened sometime in 1978. I was riding in a car with
Burt, a friend of mine, who was out of work. As we drove
along, we started discussing various career opportunities for him. He eventually asked me what my long-term
plans were. I was with Hydril Company, an oilfield service and supply firm, in a staff function, which I had held
for four years. My job, as a Program Manager, involved
facilitating the introduction of new products. In that capacity, I had a lot of interaction with high- and mid-level
management in all the functions of the company.

Burt said, "You know, at some point you've got to get
some line experience. Have you thought about working
in the plant, or seeking a position in the finance department? What about sales or engineering?"

As I considered all these suggestions, my response was
something like, "Well, I've worked with those manufacturing guys. All they think about is getting more stuff out
the door and they hate anything new. I don't think I'd enjoy it. Finance? Those guys are weird, even their mothers
don't understand them. Sales? All they do is go drinking

with their customers so they'll buy from them. I've done engineering work. The thought of sitting at a drawing board or behind a desk the rest of my life is depressing."

At this point in the conversation I was starting to feel threatened because there didn't seem to be a lot of jobs that I would enjoy. I also thought Burt might start considering me a malcontent. He then said two words that changed my life. "Jerry," he said, "Have you ever thought about *sales engineering*? What you would do is sell technical products to engineers and purchasing folks."

It was as if a light went on and the hosts of heaven were singing. "Man, Burt, I bet I could do that. I enjoy getting up in front of people and I like discussing technical things. My former boss at the company is coming to my house for dinner this Saturday night and I'll ask him about it."

During the course of a meal that weekend with Chuck and his wife, I broached the subject with him. He thought it was a great idea and said he'd help me find a position somewhere in the company. That next week, things started moving fast. Chuck was highly thought of in the organization and he discreetly mentioned my name to influential people in all three of the company's divisions. Before too long, I fielded calls from all of them wanting to discuss opportunities with me.

This book is my attempt to explain why I have had a thirty-year love affair with sales engineering (or technical sales, if you prefer). I've found it to be a rewarding profession both personally and financially. At times it can be very challenging.

A web site in the UK, www.prospects.ac.uk, gives the

following description about what the work of a typical sales engineering position might entail:

- searching for new clients that could benefit from company products or services and maximising customer potential in designated regions;
- travelling to visit potential clients;
- establishing new and maintaining existing long-term rapports with customers;
- managing and interpreting customer requirements—listening to clients and using astute questioning to understand, anticipate and exceed their needs;
- persuading clients that a product or service will best satisfy their needs in terms of quality, price and delivery;
- calculating client quotations;
- negotiating tender and contract terms, to meet both client and company needs;
- negotiating and closing sales by agreeing terms and conditions;
- offering after-sales support services;
- administering client accounts;
- analysing costs and sales;
- preparing reports for head office;
- meeting regular sales targets;
- recording and maintaining client contact data;
- co-ordinating sales projects;
- supporting marketing activities by attending trade shows, conferences and other marketing events;
- performing technical presentations and demonstrating how a product will meet client needs;
- providing pre-sales technical assistance and product education;

- liaising with other members of the sales team and other technical experts;
- solving client problems;
- helping in the design of custom-made products;
- providing training and producing support material for other members of the sales team.

This is an excellent description about some of the tasks that a sales engineer might be called upon to perform. There are a few resources like this that tell you what a sales engineer does, but I have not found any book that explains how a sales engineer actually performs these tasks. In this volume I provide a number of suggestions and hints and explain why I have found them to be helpful. I discuss some of the technical features of products I have represented to provide a feel for the types of items a sales engineer might sell. There are a number of roles that a sales engineer can fill. In the course of relating my experiences in historical order, I describe some of the various positions I've had as well as methods I've used to actually do many of the tasks listed above.

The back of the book contains a topical index showing where you can find explanations about what to do in certain selling situations, why certain aspects of technical selling are important and a description of the various roles a sales engineer might play.

1
My First Sales Engineering Assignment

If you're speaking and not getting a reaction, well, you are just making a speech.

—Author Unknown

As I mentioned in the introduction, I was presented with several opportunities in a technical sales function with Hydril with whom I had held a staff job for four years. After weighing the various job offers, I decided that the best one involved the promotion of a rather complicated hydraulic valve. In my previous position with the company, I had helped launch this product line and a division had recently been formed to manufacture and market it. In accepting this job I agreed to move from Houston to New Orleans. This was appealing at the time since most of our extended family lived there.

This type of valve is called a surface controlled subsurface safety valve and is required by federal law to be placed 100´ below the mud line in any subsea oil or gas well. It is a part of the tubing string and is held open by means of hydraulic pressure being applied to one or more lines from the surface. It is designed to fail in the safe mode, in that loss of hydraulic pressure due to a fire or some sort of unusual event, will cause the well to be shut in. The valve has to be of a slim design to fit in the well and must be able to withstand high flow rates and corrosion. It must close when pressure is removed and cannot leak. It should have the capability to receive a wireline-conveyed backup valve that will work off of its hydraulics until the tubing can be pulled and another valve run into the hole.

Needless to say, there was a lot to learn. Since my wife stayed in Houston while we tried to sell our house, I had plenty of time to learn the product, how it operated, what materials it was made of, etc. I wanted to be successful and I realized the former person who had held this position had been fired for lack of results. I decided I'd better learn as much as possible about it, and competitive valves, as fast as possible. The company didn't offer any technical or sales training at that time but they did have a working scale model made of transparent plastic so you could see the parts operating. It gave me a great deal of satisfaction to be able to explain how this piece of equipment worked and to compare it to our competitors' products.

First Selling Experiences

After a few weeks, I was ready to make sales calls. I had a few names of contacts at a number of oil companies, so I called them in order to introduce myself. Most seemed receptive and I was able to set up several appointments. All of a sudden, I realized I didn't know where their various offices were located. As sales guys in other departments helped me sort this out, I came to understand that knowing the geographic layout of the various accounts within a territory is a part of the sales engineer's discipline. I learned that you can make your life a lot less hectic if you bundle appointments geographically. Of course, you want to sequence as many contacts at a given company as possible, but it helps to know where other clients' firms are located so you can also visit them and save travel time.

I was able to uncover some experienced engineering customers who took pity on a rather green sales representative. They were helpful in giving me advice about their companies' needs and in providing names of other personnel within their respective organizations who might want to hear what I had to say. Some of my initial contacts began to function as coaches to me. I've found over the years that it is important to find someone like that who will give you information and provide help in guiding the sales process through the mine fields of an account.

New sales people are usually nervous and experience sales calls that don't turn out very well. I remember inviting my best contact at my largest account to lunch at a very nice restaurant. I talked a little fast and was demonstrative in my hand gestures. During the course of the meal, I inadvertently knocked over my water glass in the general direction of my customer. Waiters came out of the woodwork to sop up the water, remove the dishes and put on another clean linen tablecloth. My customer was a real gentleman and didn't even acknowledge my clumsiness … until I did it again ten minutes later!

My life insurance agent's first call began with him knocking on the door of a home wanting to speak to the head of the household. The lady who came to the door tearfully mentioned that she didn't need any life insurance for her husband as he had just died. I have a friend at an oilfield equipment company who was told early in his career to hand out fountain pens with the company's logo on them. Being a little inexperienced, he was very proud of the fact that he had an appointment with a man who was hard to see and with whom his company had done no prior business. He handed the man the pen only to have him pull off the top and get doused with black ink. The customer threw the pen in the trash can and said that if the pen was indicative of the quality of my friend's products, he would not do business with them. These sorts of things happen to everyone and provide good fodder for sales stories in later years.

Knowing where one's customers are located within an assigned territory comes into play in setting up sales calls for the week. The method I use begins by developing a list of the people I need to see and then ranking them. If someone is an important client I might start by inviting him to lunch. After all the lunches or other special events are scheduled, I then contact other customers and try to set up appointments considering where they are located within my territory and where I'll be during the week. This maximizes the use of my time and minimizes the costs to my company for fuel for my car.

I've learned to allow plenty of time for travel, and if it looks like I'm going to be late, I promptly contact my customer. Both of these actions can reduce stress. Early in my career, I was made well aware of this while running late one morning as I was leaving my house. I was carrying a rather large cup of hot coffee with the intention of placing it in the cup holder of the car. Unfortunately, my hand hit the steering wheel as I was getting in and I spilled coffee on my pants. Reaching over to get a paper towel in the front seat, I spilled even more on myself. In anger, I tossed the plastic cup out the open door only to have it ricochet off the wall of my house back in my lap. Needless to say, this was on a Monday.

Territory management is especially important if your sales responsibilities include out-of-town travel. I have a file of maps from rental car companies for the various cities that I visit and have marked on them where my customers are located. I have found that contacts are a little more open to seeing out-of-town sales personnel but I've learned to be cognizant about where they are located to optimize my schedule.

Training

My company began to offer a training course on sales and product presentations. They stressed a method called FAB, which stood for Features, Advantages, and

Benefits. They taught us to present a feature about the product, how that resulted in an advantage to the customer and then how it benefited them. In my case, the valve had two lines (feature), it could be set very deep because of hydraulic balancing (advantage), and the benefit was that you didn't have to concern yourself with putting bigger springs in it the deeper you went.

It is my understanding that a lot of companies were subscribing to the FAB presentation technique back in the 1970s and 1980s. I liked this method because it was relatively easy to demonstrate to my customers a number of features about our product and how that would help them. (Because it was sometimes difficult to distinguish between an advantage and a benefit, the technique was later renamed FFB for Feature, Function, Benefit. The focus shifted to what it is, what it does, and what it does for the customer.)

We were trained to carefully observe the office of a prospective customer to ascertain what type of person he was. Did he have pictures of his family on the wall or plaques displaying his accomplishments? Were there trophies of fishing contests or golf tournaments? What did she talk about and in what manner did she say things? All these clues helped tailor our presentation to best match what to say and how to say it. (To this day, I casually survey a person's office to determine what is important to him or her. People like talking about what is of interest to them, and I try to steer the conversation so as to build rapport through common interests. People also like to do business with people who are like them.)

At the end of one of these weeklong training sessions,

we were called upon to make a presentation about our product in front of the other trainees and the instructors. I gave a lot of thought about the personalities of the trainers (who were the judges) and changed my usual presentation on the valve to best reflect its features and benefits considering the use of terms more in sync with their character. I won the contest, received a nice trophy, and I left the training with a renewed passion for making presentations.

Because I had spent so much time studying our valve, I could easily talk for an hour about how it worked, what it was made of, its features and many other details. Being an engineer by training, I loved discussing these technical issues. Unfortunately, I noticed that I could bore people if the features I presented did not solve a problem for them. Looking back on it, I was trying to show off my knowledge instead of making a sale.

In the course of time, I learned that the most well-received presentations occurred when I discovered some hot button issue for the client before I gave the talk. For instance, if they had experienced a recent failure of a competitor's valve, I'd stress our excellent performance record, the tests we'd done or name-drop other companies who were using our product.

Modern training methods by companies like the Sandler Sales Institute and Neuromarketing Inc., promote this effective technique. They refer to it as "finding the customer's pain." It could be some technical issue that a feature of my product solves or it could be something commercial like pricing or delivery. Some techniques focus on the positive reasons why a given contact within a company might want to buy my product. For example, an up-and-coming young engineer might be willing to take a chance on purchasing from me as opposed to the established supplier because it might enhance his career. Another training organization, Miller-Heiman, uses this method and has an elaborate spreadsheet for handling sales for big projects.

In any case, it makes sense to analyze what might motivate your customer to purchase your product and concentrate your discussion in those areas first. As engineers and technical personnel, we must resist the urge to use the podium to display how smart we are by presenting a mind-numbing list of features and details.

There is a lot to be said about mirroring your presentation or sales technique to the person you are addressing. I once called on a drilling rig superintendent who was not very talkative. However, I noticed that he had sayings in his office about why value is important. Because what I was offering was more expensive than the current product he was using, I stressed the increased value that his company would receive because of the features of my product. I was successful in making the first of many sales to his company.

Another aspect of mirroring is to dress appropriately for the audience. Back then, we wore a coat and tie when calling on oil company personnel located in downtown New Orleans. When we went across the Mississippi River to the west bank, we wore a golf shirt.

Is your customer a results-oriented person or a laid-back individual? Does the challenge of understanding something very involved motivate him, or is he a bigger-than-life person wanting people to know that he is the boss? There are many different ways that people have tried to understand and categorize human personality. They usually involve four basic character types as well as mixtures of them. The initial study of this subject goes back to the Greek doctor Hippocrates, who delineated four different behavior types based upon mistaken observations of the color of their blood as seen through their skin. He segregated people by the red-blooded, damn the torpedoes types (the sanguine), those motivated by accomplishing things (the choleric), the knowledge-oriented individuals (the melancholy), and the easy-going, laid-back types (the phlegmatic). There are now personality studies that assign colors, animals, and a myriad of other methods of attempting to understand what motivates people and makes them act certain ways.

I once called on a man who I discerned had a choleric type of personality. When he allowed me in his office, he indicated he didn't have a lot of time for me to talk to him. I said it would only take five minutes, and then he watched me set the timer on my calculator. I began to give my talk and when the alarm went off, he laughed, ignored it and proceeded to ask me many questions about my product. I left thirty minutes later and shortly thereafter made the first of many sales to him.

There is a continual need to learn as much as possible about our customers, the industry, our products and that of the competition. Regular attendance at professional meetings can be a good way of learning more about new things in your chosen industry. It is also a convenient way of seeing customers and demonstrating commitment to the industry.

Some sales engineers are professionally registered in the state(s) where they practice. They have passed an Engineer in Training (EIT) test shortly before or after graduating from college and must demonstrate proficiency in their discipline through work and positive references after a few years into their career. They are then eligible to take the Professional Practices test. Professional Engineers (PE's) in most states are required to take a certain number of professional development hours (PDH) on an annual basis and to keep records of such activity.

The advantage of becoming a PE might not seem evident at first to someone involved in selling. However, I have found it to be a vehicle to establish credibility with my customers, and something unique that they will remember about me. It has allowed me entrance into opportunities that I might not have had without it. I once gave a half-hour technical discussion to a group of client engineers and was surprised when one of the higher-up attendees emailed me wanting a letter from me certifying that he attended the session. He was using my talk to help satisfy his continuing education unit (CEU) requirements. Since then, I have used that need to email PE's about upcoming talks by others and myself. On a couple of occasions, I have been asked by clients to serve as a technical reference for them when they applied for their PE license.

Most large companies offer in-house training programs or will allow individual or group participation at off-site venues. These can be technical or selling oriented functions. I have attended motivational sessions—at my own expense—by speakers such as Zig Ziglar and have found them to be very helpful. However, in some cases, we should be discerning about what sort of motivational training is being offered. I was once in a department of technical sales personnel who were subjected to a most humiliating eight hours of presentations. The speaker had us hollering out "I'm the best!" in ever increasing volume for extended periods. This was more oriented for consumer sales and not for highly specialized professional sales personnel.

My discussion about training would not be complete unless I related the following story. I once worked with two sales guys named Ron and David who were always playing practical jokes on each other. On one occasion, we all had to go out of town for a company training session. As David was checking into the hotel, he was told by the registration clerk (who was in on the scheme) that she had no record of him having completed his pre-work for the upcoming class. He got irritated and complained that this was another example of the company not communicating properly. She said that she did happen to have a copy of the test he had to take and if he would sit in the lobby and finish it, he'd then be eligible to register. David then dutifully sat there with a #2 pencil and worked on the "pre-work" that Ron had previously made up. Meanwhile Ron and some other coworkers were laughing hilariously in a side lobby.

The Product Offering

While in New Orleans, I was successful in developing a number of new accounts. These were typically large oil companies who liked one or more features of our valve. The operation of our product involved the downward motion of a flow tube, which was caused by hydraulic pressure being applied to it. As it moved down, it pushed against a ball with a hole in the center of it. Because there were off center pins on the outside of the ball, which rode in slots, it caused the ball to rotate open as it moved down. When hydraulic pressure was removed, a helical spring pushed a flow tube under the ball upward, thus causing it to rotate to the closed position. This design resulted in a rather compact valve with a relatively small outside diameter (OD) for a given size of tubing.

We had competition from a design involving a flapper that was pushed open as a flow tube moved downward and slid past it. It was not quite as compact and required the addition of more springs to overcome the hydraulic head if the valve were to be placed deeper. However, in the course of time the competition found ways of overcoming these obstacles. Their price was less expensive and I then learned that no product is perfect. The advantage of our second hydraulic line was countered by the fact that we had more failure modes because our product was more complicated.

It was a lesson to me that the actual item we are selling, in most cases, is a small part of the overall product offering. Some of the other things we may be providing include less failure modes, better track record, higher ratings, more features, packaging, faster delivery, industry certification, annual rebates, quantity discounts, free service, and many other items. The product knowledge of the sales engineer and his or her ability to assist in after-the-sale delivery issues may even be a consideration by the customer.

I have had situations where one of the most important issues to the customer was an intangible performance measurement of the company. Big clients are always concerned about liability and the particular matter in one instance was our safety record. Intuitively, one would think it would be a measure of the recordable safety incidents while installing the equipment at their location. However, they wanted our overall record including these figures as well as those at our manufacturing facility. They were trying to determine the level of our company's commitment to safety. I was able to give them a one-page sheet displaying this data, which incidentally, showed a better safety record than theirs!

Other intangible things that clients might want to know include the company's quality program, environmental record, or capital expenditure plans. Part of the sales engineer's job involves uncovering what might be important to the customer and presenting the product offering in the best light.

Sometimes discussions of products revolve around quality and grade issues. Quality has to do with getting what you are expecting. There are more than 500 million references on the internet about this subject. If we buy a hamburger from Burger King we expect it to taste good, the bun to be fresh, and the pickles and lettuce to look a certain way. Whether the hamburger is purchased in Los Angeles, New York, or Detroit, we assume all these expectations will be met.

Product grade has to do more with features and performance. For instance, we might expect the same quality whether we buy a Cadillac or a Chevrolet. However, the Cadillac has more features, rides better, is quieter, and is more comfortable. We may actually be doing our customer a disservice by selling him the more expensive Cadillac because he may only need a Chevrolet. One could argue that the Cadillac is a better car and whatever the Chevrolet can do, it can do better. However, it costs more. In business, the customer could take the money saved by buying the more appropriate Chevrolet and use it to invest in a productive piece of equipment and increase his company's profitability.

Being Unique

Because I started studying our competitor's valves more closely, and in the process, developed a lot of technical information, I thought it might be interesting to write an article about this subject. It would set me apart as being unique and would enhance my credibility. Trade journals are always looking for copy to put in their magazines. I contacted the editor of one of these organs and he was interested in such an article, perhaps also because our company had ads in his magazine.

It took longer to write than I had planned. In addition, I had to submit some drawings with it in order to explain how these types of valves worked. The article came out in May 1980, and I would like to say I was instantly famous, but that would be a lie. In fact, the only feedback from my company was questioning why I had chosen that magazine versus another they would have preferred.

However, writing the article helped me logically explain the features of the various designs of these valves. I was perceived as being credible when I handed out copies of the article when doing subsequent presentations. My company got free publicity by virtue of its name being shown as my employer in the title and the biographical sketch. In addition, it gave me a feeling of accomplishment. I will more fully address the subject of being unique in a later chapter.

Product Management

The oil industry began having a rough time in the early 1980s and Hydril started feeling the effects. The service sector usually has wild swings in its profitability. When things are good, they are really good. When bad ...well, you get the picture. Those segments of my company involving drilling equipment started having a downturn. Hydril had never had a layoff in its fifty-three year history but it became necessary to conduct a reduction-in-force, or RIF as it is called.

As can be imagined, some of the staff functions were first trimmed back. Then those involved in the slowest part of the business, drilling equipment, experienced the loss of a few people. There were some high level personnel involved with tubing and casing who were let go, especially because they had not foreseen a huge inventory build-up and had continued to recommend the acquisition of new and very expensive machinery.

About this time, my group also started experiencing a slowdown. In addition, we started getting complaints from the field that at relatively shallow depths and in certain environments, our valves would not close. Since the primary function of this equipment is to shut off the flow of hydrocarbons in an emergency situation, this was a serious concern. We also needed to have certain periodic qualification tests done on our valve, and our manufacturing group was not being responsive to having that done. Finally, there were rumors floating around that our division was for sale.

In the midst of all these challenges, the company decided to transfer my family back to Houston. We had been in New Orleans for three years and I had been promoted to a district supervisor position. My new title was Product Manager and, in order to address the valve malfunction problem, several engineers were assigned to help me on a part-time basis.

We investigated the action of the valve during the closing sequence and determined that the biggest cause of the problem was that there was high internal friction generated by the valve's seals. Certain environments, especially those with high cuts of hot water caused the seals to swell. We studied various seal materials and concluded that a high durometer Viton would be resistant to that and would have a lower coefficient of friction relative to the sliding parts of the valve. We recommended that change along with several other ones and presented our findings to our management and then to our biggest customer. They agreed with our conclusions and the changes were made.

The potential sale of our division was particularly vexing because some of the employees involved in the negotiations were friends of mine. We all knew we had jobs to do and could not talk about this so we carefully avoided each other. It was a demotivator for all of us in the division but the problem was solved because no one wanted to buy the group at the price being proposed. So, all the personnel were transferred to a new division that incorporated all the non-core businesses of the company.

The qualification testing of the seals became a political issue as the group involved with the manufacture of the valve was physically located far away from our management and felt like the test was unsafe to perform. We had had it done several years prior to this, but the person who had performed it had left the company. The test involved subjecting the seals to diesel fluid at a temperature above its flash point. After repeated requests to get this done, I thought I could embarrass them into doing it by telling them if they didn't do it, I'd come out there and do it myself. They called my bluff.

So, shortly after that I found myself alone in the back yard of the West Coast manufacturing facility with a closed container of hot diesel in which I had previously immersed the seals. The trick was to run a steel tube from the container so that the other end was setting in a bath of cold diesel. This would allow the diesel to expand but not be exposed to air. After a tense hour, armed with a fire extinguisher, I shut off the heater and let it cool down. We examined the seals for dimensional changes and then certified that we had successfully passed the test.

Summary

There are many different things that a sales engineer must do in order to be successful. He serves as the eyes and ears of the company in seeking out new opportunities and in advising about product line extensions. I was once in the unenviable position of having to tell a customer that the higher pressure rating valve that we had promised him was not available. He hung up on me. I had previously alerted my management that he would not be happy about this. Among other things, we may have to take on the role of a customer advocate within our own company to satisfy the marketplace.

The sales territory for which I was responsible had about a dozen accounts, all oil companies. Of those companies, there were sixty to seventy engineers or operational personnel who could specify our equipment. Because I spent a lot of time educating my customers on these types of valves and the features and benefits of our equipment, this selling experience was most like being a teacher. I did use a referral technique in helping to bolster sales because many of these companies were partners in other wells and shared information. I interfaced with our service personnel because there was some ancillary equipment that needed to be added to the valves before they went downhole. I also apprised complementary equipment manufacturers when our valve was specified, so that their hardware would easily accommodate our control lines.

I relied on mechanics and hydraulics in understanding how the valve worked and in attempting to explain it to others. A knowledge of materials—both metal and elastomeric—was helpful in this job, as well as failure analysis.

I found the work challenging and I left this opportunity with a better understanding about how to present the features and benefits of my product offering after determining what the customer actually needed. I also realized that no product is perfect and will not satisfy all the technical, commercial and intangible needs of all customers.

2
Another Opportunity

A salesman minus enthusiasm is just a clerk.
—Harry F. Banks, sales trainer

I served as a Product Manager for about six months and then was made aware of an opportunity in another division whose business was to machine the ends of pipe for use in oil and gas wells. (Some wells can be as deep as 35,000´. On a clear day, if you notice a jet flying above, it typically cruises at about that height above the ground.)

Oilfield Pipe

Most tubing in a hydrocarbon producing well ranges in size from 2⅜" to 4½" in diameter and is suspended from the wellhead the entire depth of the well. The threads allow the pipe to be screwed together in approximately 32´ sections and provide mechanical and pressure integrity. Along its length and throughout its life, the pipe can be subjected to varying amounts of tension, compression, internal pressure, external pressure, bending, torque, and thermal shock. The tubing is the conduit for the hydrocarbons and because it is not cemented in place, it can be removed from the well at a later date and possibly reused.

Casing is larger diameter pipe whose functions are to prevent the well from caving in, to isolate different zones from one another and to serve as a backup safety pressure vessel in the event the tubing leaks. There can be many different strings of casing in a well, one inside the other. There are a variety of reasons for this, including the fact that you can only drill so deep before you come to a zone that might cause a cave in of the hole. Casing is usually run in 42′ to 44′ lengths.

Most oilfield tubing and casing is joined together with API (American Petroleum Institute) threads. The design includes a coupling threaded on one end into which the threaded pipe is screwed. The API eight-round thread has eight threads per inch and the thread roots and crests are rounded to prevent stress risers. Copious amounts of thread dope are applied to the threads to help effect a seal. API connections are good enough for 80% of domestic applications.

However, depending upon a given operator's design manual, certain wells require a premium connection. Some of the conditions that trigger the use of a more elaborate thread include high pressure, deviated wells, the presence of H_2S (a poisonous gas), extremely deep wells, offshore wells, corrosion, and a number of other issues.

A premium connection typically has one or more metal-to-metal (MTM) seals and may be either coupled or of an integral design. This later design finds use in tight-hole, low clearance wells where many casing strings are run inside the other and therefore allowance for a big diameter coupling would be prohibitive.

The position of which I was made aware was to become the regional manager promoting Hydril's line of premium connections in London. The company sent my wife and me overseas to scout out housing accommodations and to determine if we would be happy with such a move. We made the trip and were very excited about this opportunity. However, shortly after this the company decided that it would be too cost prohibitive to send us there and notified me that they had another job they wanted me to take on. We were disappointed but there was not a whole lot we could do about it but to keep moving forward.

National Account Management

At that time Hydril was having a hard time managing opportunities for large projects. For instance, a major oil company was planning the development of an oilfield in Wyoming that would require premium threads on many thousands of joints. The engineering personnel who would make the decision on whose connection would be used were located in Midland, Texas. Qualification tests on each manufacturer's connection were to be done in Houston and the purchasing and management personnel involved in the acquisition and documentation were also in Houston. This project involved three salespersons operating in two regions, as well as technical personnel reporting up through the vice president of engineering.

Hydril was concerned that its personnel were not communicating on a timely basis with each other about this project, as well as other relevant matters concerning that particular account. In addition, this customer and its projects were of sufficient import to our company that our management wanted to be kept informed on a regular basis about the status of discussions, negotiations, testing, and general relationship with this major oil company.

I was appointed as the company's first National Account Manager to facilitate our sales and technical efforts with this account as well as two others. Because I needed to enlist the support of our field sales personnel, I traveled to various locations and explained what I needed and assured them I would not call on their customers without them and would keep them informed on the status of large projects. I was able to put together a rather large organizational chart on my assigned accounts showing both line and staff personnel. I sent out a monthly report that went to all the field salesmen for each account, their bosses, and our management.

The job was largely one of coordination and communication. I would use persuasion to encourage our field sales personnel to perform certain tasks to keep big projects coming in our direction. In addition I met with our engineers as well as the account's testing personnel and incorporated these discussions into my reports. Management liked this because they knew what was going on and could make decisions on a timely basis. Because of the success of this program two other employees became National Account Managers.

New Product Introduction

Shortly after this my boss suggested we meet after work for a drink. Whenever he invited me to do so I knew something was up. Over a whiskey sour, he said that the company was pleased with what I had done and wanted me to head up the introduction of a new line of connections. I was familiar with this thread, having met with the inventor and been present when it had first been run in the ground as a trial string several years prior to this.

The design was revolutionary, involving the concept of a wedge. Imagine the ends of two mating pieces machined such that a helical wedge is the only thing left on the pin and box. The leading edge of the pin is thin and becomes wider as it progresses inboard on the pipe. The box end is just the opposite. In addition, the shape of the thread is a dovetail instead of an inverted "U" as on an 8-round connection. Such a thread can exhibit very high torque ratings with great sealability. The dovetail design prevents any possibility of connection jump-out because everything is locked in place.

The company had worked on this concept for years and had kept the technology under wraps. There had been a concern that the design was so superior that it might cannibalize the existing flagship thread. The company had also been loath to patent the elements of this connection because they knew that would start the seventeen-year proprietary clock ticking. However, some of the patents on the bread and butter thread were expiring and other companies were copying it. The downturn was starting to affect this side of the business and so the decision was made to introduce this new connection as a low cost alternative. As you can imagine, however, it is not a simple matter to machine a dovetail shaped thread with varying width and to do it inexpensively.

My job, therefore, was to coordinate the rollout of this complex thread as an inexpensive connection in a down market with occasional layoffs of peer and management personnel. I loved the challenge. For more severe applications we included the possibility of a metal-to-metal seal and even an elastomeric backup seal. Connections were available on integral as well as coupled pipe.

I immediately started working with the engineering department on a catalog that would show all the sizes and weights of pipe for which the connection would be available as well as all the ratings for each. I did some sketches and met with an artist who would provide the artwork for the brochure. To demonstrate how the wedge worked we had rectangular aluminum blocks machined that were about five inches long having two mating parts that would slide into each other. We also machined a number of aluminum pipe samples of various sizes, including integral and coupled as well as incorporating both MTM and thread seal-only styles. I had both the wedges and the pipe samples anodized red and had the words "Series 500" engraved so that the letters were silver on a red background. They looked striking.

On a certain day we had all the reps and their bosses come to Houston for a sales meeting. Near the end of the session I gave a talk about the new connection and provided the salesmen and their managers with a kit containing the aluminum blocks, some hastily made brochures and some other technical information on the connection. Each region had access to a few of the pipe samples. We also announced that there would be a $500 cash prize for the salesman who got the first order. I said I'd be available to make joint sales calls with them to explain the product to their customers.

During the session I got asked some hard questions about pricing, the qualification testing that had been done on the product, availability, accessory threading, and many other issues. The salesmen left knowing there were some still unanswered questions but enthused about the product and eager to get the cash prize. We wrote up a press release and distributed it to the media.

After the salesmen left town I noticed that the wedge blocks would become jammed if they were put together too tightly. The only thing that would free them would be to strike one end on a carpeted floor. However, if you didn't hit the correct end, it would jam more tightly. I neglected to bevel some sharp corners on the block and I noticed that when it finally released after being struck the sharp corner would imbed itself in your thumb. We had sales reps all over the country with bleeding thumbs.

I started making trips and giving presentations explaining the benefits of the new connection to end-users and distributors. It was especially good for high torque applications in which tubing might be used to drill the well. Because it was on pipe that was not upset on the ends, it could be recut many times thus salvaging the pipe body. A salesman in West Texas was the first salesman to capture an order and it was my pleasure to present him with the $500 check.

I continued to work on the rollout as we added other

sizes and built up an inventory of running tools to facilitate rig operations. I assisted with the threading of accessory items that were necessary to produce the wells and worked on pricing and manufacturing support issues.

One morning I was told that there had been a deep layoff in the ranks of the sales people. The company said they had appreciated what I had done and offered me a position as a sales representative calling on oil company and distributor personnel in the Houston area. Even though this was a demotion, I was glad I had a job because many of the other oil service companies were also letting people go.

I worked in this capacity for about a year until a Monday one week before Thanksgiving in 1986. The Human Resource office called me in when I arrived at work. They provided me with an envelope with a severance check and a letter saying my services were no longer needed. I was not entirely surprised and was pleased that the severance package was larger than I had expected. After I gathered my composure I actually was relieved that it was over. I had worked for Hydril for twelve years and watched it grow from an $80 million company to almost $1 billion in revenues. From about 1982 until 1986, I saw good friends and business associates being laid off. It was like gradual amputation. The company went from about 350 employees up to 4,000 only to go back to 350 by 1986.

Hydril provided an outsourcing service that included a group session to encourage us to think about where we would go from there in our lives. I remember thinking that my ideal would be to try something a little more speculative but that would have a continuing source of steady income.

Summary

In most of my assignments during this phase of my career, I worked through other individuals. Because I had been in sales before, I was cognizant of the ownership that an individual salesperson feels about his accounts. I let them know that I was there to assist them and I appreciated the job they were doing. I always discussed the objectives of an individual call with them before visiting their accounts so we would work together as a team.

Because I did presentations introducing the wedge thread, public speaking was also an important part of this job.

I relied on a basic understanding of mechanics in describing and providing sketches of the features of the wedge thread. Some knowledge of geometry and statics was also helpful.

I learned a lot about advertising, product introductions, working through other salespersons and giving technical presentations during these three years. I realized that you had to be flexible when working in a large company and to not be disappointed when things did not turn out as you might have expected. All you can do is your best.

3
Long-Term Consulting

A problem well stated is a problem half solved.
—Charles F. Kettering, inventor

A friend of mine heard that I had been laid off and called to say he would see if he could get me on as a consultant with the company he worked for. Among other things the firm performed qualification testing on pipe and oilfield connections. Meanwhile, I started sending out resumés, networking, and looking in the newspaper's classifieds for job opportunities.

Things were not promising in Houston at that time and any oilfield experience was actually looked down upon. I kept track of all the opportunities that looked promising and went on some interviews. I put a probability percent rating next to each one and kept a day-by-day total of the sum of all of them. I arbitrarily decided that when the sum equaled 500% that I would probably have something worthwhile to do.

I remember my family's baby sitter observing that my attitude seemed upbeat in the midst of not having a job. I appreciated the compliment, but I had no choice except to remain optimistic. We had three small children, two car payments, a house payment, and a wife who did not work outside the home. I could not afford the luxury of being depressed or angry about the situation.

Qualification Testing

I did go in for an interview with my friend's company, H.O. Mohr Research and Engineering, whose primary customers were oil and oil service companies. As can be imagined, their business was not very good at the time and they figured that I could probably sell their testing service to my former employer and its competitors. Some of my friends ended up working for Japanese steel companies who were eager to have their premium connections qualified in the United States. Harvey Mohr said that I could work for his company for the two weeks before Christmas and if I could sell anything they'd talk with me after the holidays about something more permanent.

I wasn't able to actually book anything for them during that time but I did uncover a number of promising opportunities and I made it a point to keep accurate notes of my activities. When I came back after the holidays, they said they'd try it for another week and to talk with them on Friday about continuing the arrangement. We operated like that for a few weeks and I did turn in some small sales. After a while I quit going back on Fridays and just kept showing up on Mondays. During this time I kept interviewing with other companies.

I saw an ad for a manufacturer's representative firm who wanted someone to sell packaging and material handling equipment into the downstream petroleum and petrochemical industries. This seemed to be a good way to complement the spikes in the oil industry and level load my income. However, this opportunity was a straight commission arrangement with all business expenses to my account.

I suddenly realized that this was just what I had envisioned, a speculative opportunity coupled with something offering steady income. I met with Harvey Mohr and said I'd like to work for him on a more flexible schedule of about three to four days per week and would field calls from him and his customers even when I wasn't being paid. He liked the concept because he was negotiating to buy back his company from some investors and money was tight. I bought a cell phone, which at that time cost $850, and it was installed permanently in my car.

I agreed to work for the other company, Choctaw Sales, on a part-time basis and explained to them what I was doing to augment my income. They thought that was a wonderful idea because they knew it would take some time for me to generate sales for them.

These were tough times and I found myself waking up in the middle of the night, sweating and worried, dreaming that I had my family on the edge of a cliff financially. The consultant job at Mohr only paid about half of what I had been formerly making. There was this constant tension between receiving small but sure compensation from Mohr versus making much more money at Choctaw but on a speculative basis. My office at Mohr was an air-conditioned hut inside of a large metal building that served as the test lab. One morning I poured sugar from a cylindrical container into my coffee cup and a roach also came out. It was easy to find things to get depressed about, but I couldn't afford to let that happen.

Well, I began to book some sales for H. O. Mohr. Qualification tests for a given size, weight, and grade of an oilfield connection can easily run $100,000. Many of the large oil companies have very elaborate protocols which may involve as many as twelve highly engineered samples with the elements of the thread (taper, thread engagement, seal interference, etc.) designed at the minimum and maximum ends of the tolerance band. These qualifications can also include exposing the connection to various combinations of tension, compression, internal and external pressure, bending, temperature, and thermal shock.

My job was to determine which connection manufacturer needed to have a test performed and then to solicit a bid. I also was responsible for doing the quotes, which I did based upon the amount of time and manpower the test required as well as the use of test equipment we rented. The primary piece of machinery we utilized to do the tension and compression loading was a 3,000,000-pound rated test frame consisting of two very thick plates pushed apart or pulled together by a number of hydraulic cylinders. By adding optional equipment, we could subject casing samples to bending, external pressure, and elevated temperatures. The company relied on my expertise on the quotes and some of the larger projects could cost $300,000.

In the course of time I became involved in testing many

different pieces of equipment, most of them from the oil industry. Some of the projects involved destructive tests in tension or pressure. We once were called upon to blow up a piece of pipe with 36,000 psi of hydraulic pressure. We also tested mooring chains, underwater pipelines, traveling blocks, fiberglass pipe, anchors, hydraulic umbilicals, and many other items. In some cases we applied strain gages to the parts and used this to measure the imposed strains and calculate the stresses. I quoted some of these programs on a time-and-materials basis and some as fixed cost, depending upon the customer's desire.

One of the most unusual tests I was called upon to quote began with a call from another testing outfit, our cross-town rival. They said someone who wanted to pressure test a vessel to destruction had contacted them. They were not interested in pursuing it and had suggested the client contact me. The customer called and explained that he wanted to test a commercial gas bottle, the type used to contain welding gases. He wanted to burst it with gas and estimated that it would take 10,000 psi. When I calculated the amount of gas involved I realized that we had a potential rocket on our hands. We looked at different ways of doing the procedure and had the customer agree that if we could partially fill it with water we would do the test.

We had a 5,000 psi rated pressure horizontal vessel on-site that was 42" ID and 20′ long. We first welded a flat ¼" plate to the end of a 30" diameter pipe we had on hand and then loaded that into the vessel. We placed the gas bottle inside of the pipe and then welded another plate to the open end of this pipe. There was enough space above the plate for us to pass a pressure line from the gas bottle and threaded that though a port on the lid of the chamber and then closed it. We partially filled the chamber with water and then proceeded to pressure up the gas bottle.

When the gas bottle split open around 10,000 psi there was a noise like a freight train and then water shot fifty feet in the air through a relief port in the chamber. When we opened the chamber we saw where the bottle had hit the front plate, ricocheted backward and hit the back plate, and ended up by the front plate. There were dents along the length of the inside of the 30″ pipe. The gas bottle had a crack along its length. The customer was pleased.

Another aspect of this job was to entertain clients and keep them occupied if there were problems or delays as we were performing a procedure. I remember one particular instance when we were having a hard time getting up to test pressure on a certain piece of equipment. The lab manager called me and asked me to talk to the two customer representatives who were on-site to witness the test. I walked them around the lab and the boneyard in the back and showed them the remains of underwater pipe we had smashed, casing we had pulled to destruction, a casing spider we had cracked, and many other items, all the while filling them in on all the details of what had happened when the parts failed. As we were walking back to witness their test, one of the clients paused and asked, "What type of childhood did you have?"

Expert Witnessing

I have to admit that breaking things and getting paid to do it was a lot of fun. We got a call from a third party wanting us to pull some full-length samples of fiberglass pipe to destruction. We had a vertical tower that could generate the type of loads that were required so I presented a quote to him. He neglected to tell me that the test results were to be used in a lawsuit. An American company had produced some fiberglass pipe and it had been sold to a Chinese company through a third party. When the pipe had been put in the well it failed and at much lower values than the specifications.

On the day of the test our parking lot was inundated with late model luxury vehicles driven by attorneys representing both sides of the litigation. They climbed all over our test frame and asked innumerable questions. We did the test, wrote up the results and sent a report to our client. I was happy that it was over.

However, about a week later I was notified by letter that I was to be deposed. (That was news to me because I was not a king and had no desire to be one.) They wanted me to go to downtown Houston, bring remnants of the test specimens and present a deposition. They said they'd pay our company for my time. When I got down there, the opposing attorneys introduced themselves and the court reporter and then swore me in. I have never been asked so many questions so fast in all my life. I answered them succinctly and truthfully and was excused.

Our invoice to the attorney's firm who had called me went unpaid for about six months. Calls to their office were not returned. However, one night they called my home and said they might need me to travel to Dallas the next day and give another deposition there. I agreed to go but waited until all the arrangements had been made the next day and then said, "You know, our invoice has not been paid, and we're reluctant for me to spend any more time on this project." The courier arrived within two hours with a check.

On this trip the two attorneys again asked all sorts of questions, much of which I had answered previously. They made motions back and forth and things seemed a little tense between them. However, after the session was over, the two opposing lawyers and I shared a cab and had a wonderful discussion about sports, the weather, and our families.

Several months went by and they said I needed to appear in a Dallas civil courtroom as an expert witness. I arrived the night before the trial and had dinner with the attorneys representing the Chinese. They showed me a deposition given by an expert witness on the other side as well as his comments on my deposition. I was shocked to see that their witness was not only an acquaintance of mine but an internationally known expert on fiberglass pipe and an occasional client of our company. Intimidated, I spent several hours going over what he had said and how I might counter it. Fortunately, it was not hard to do and I couldn't wait to appear in court.

The next day, I met the attorneys for breakfast and then they escorted me to the courthouse. They told me to cool my heels on a bench outside the courtroom until they called me in. I spent three entertaining hours watching couples applying for marriage licenses before I was called. I was introduced and then sworn in. They wanted my name and address and asked me some very difficult questions along the line of, "What does an engineer do and how does he do it?" After three minutes of this, both sides rested and the judge said I was excused. I looked at the attorney for the Chinese and he nodded as if to say, "Leave." I was so disappointed because I wanted to share all my wisdom with the U.S. judicial system.

I waited about twenty minutes for the attorney to come outside to talk to me but he never did and I never saw him again. I did correspond with the attorney for the other side, offering our services in future litigation as expert witnesses. Later, I found out that earlier in the day of the trial there had been some talk about settling this lawsuit out of court and apparently they did.

Getting Paid

Because H.O. Mohr was a small company, it was critical that the management have a good feel for the amount of business that had been booked, when we might perform it, and what other opportunities were forthcoming. To provide this information, I did a monthly forecast and listed every project of which I was aware. I multiplied the percentage possibility that we would capture each one by the dollar amount it represented and then put that amount in the column corresponding to the month that we would complete it.

Cash flow was another important issue. I feel that it is good for the sales engineer to get involved when the client to whom he sold a project has not paid on a timely basis. In many cases he can be more influential in getting this resolved than can accounting or management personnel.

We had sold several testing projects to a connection manufacturer and I was made aware that they owed us $150,000 and it was more than ninety days old. I had several engineering friends at that company and they were embarrassed about this and knew that we would be unwilling to perform any more work for them. One of them suggested that we meet for lunch and he would bring their controller along. It was a very profitable lunch. I paid $25 for us to break bread and the controller slipped me a check for $15,000 on the oldest work we had done for them. He said to give him a call in a few weeks and he'd see what he could do to whittle the outstanding amount down further.

I met for lunch on a number of occasions with the controller. He'd give me checks ranging from $5,000 to $12,000. When the amount owed got down to $75,000, their management discovered what he was doing and told him to stop. We ultimately got paid but it took a threatened lawsuit and another two years.

On another occasion, a company wanted us to pull an undersea umbilical to destruction. This is a bundled package of hydraulic hoses and, in some cases, electric lines, that is used to control the valves on a subsea wellhead. The umbilical can be 8″ or more in diameter and be rather cumbersome and heavy to handle. It is not very flexible. I worked up a time-and-materials quote based upon the information they had given me about the lengths of the sample umbilicals they wanted to pull apart. Part of my job was the preliminary engineering of these tests and costing out whatever fixturing would be required to accomplish it.

Unfortunately, the dimensions of the sample lengths they had provided were not accurate and we spent quite a bit of time and money rigging up for the tests, as well as providing additional fixturing. We apprised them verbally that there would be some extra costs and their engineer agreed to pay whatever was necessary to get the job done on a timely basis. We completed the work and sent them an invoice. During the course of six months I repeatedly called them to inquire about when they planned on paying it.

I finally went with Harvey Mohr and met with the client's general manager. We let him vent about the cost overruns and then explained that we did the work as requested and that their inaccurate dimensions were the cause of the additional work. What made this somewhat difficult was that the engineer whom I had worked with had left their company. The manager complained some more and then I laid a breakdown of the costs of this project on his desk and politely said that we would like to continue to work for them but we needed to get this resolved.

About this time I saw him looking down at the numbers and he became quiet. I knew that he was contemplating what he should do next. I also realized that whoever talked next would lose this discussion and I determined that I would not say anything and that it was his move. Out the corner of my eye, I could see that Harvey was getting ready to say something, so I very gently kicked him. There was a continued quiet and then I heard Harvey breathe in as if he was going to say something again. I kicked him harder. He looked at me like I was crazy and I carefully put my finger next to my lips. He got the message and the client suddenly agreed to pay us half of the disputed amount immediately and the balance in thirty days.

Later in my career, I was with a company that was owed more than $500,000 by its biggest client, most of it aged more than ninety days. I talked to my purchasing and engineering contacts within that company and all they could say is that they were instituting a new accounting program and that they were behind in their payments. Through networking with companies that sold complementary equipment, I discovered that they too were not getting their payments on a timely basis. I mentioned this issue to one of their representatives after a technical meeting held at the client's office. He said, "Come with me," and introduced me to the lady who processed all the paperwork for my customer. It was obvious she needed more help to do this work. When I inquired why it was taking so long to get paid she asked for the name of my company. She explained that she was handling the paperwork in alphabetical order and because my company's name began with a "V" it would be a while before we got paid.

That was about the silliest way for deciding when payments would be forthcoming that I'd ever heard and I made my sentiments known to my customer. I also made it a point to occasionally go by the lady's office and bring her promotional items that we gave to the engineers. All of the money was paid within a month and we thereafter rarely had more than $10,000 older than thirty days with that account.

It is important for the sales engineer to get involved in these types of situations because he knows the client best and his career is dependent upon good relations between the client and the company he works for. In some cases there may be a misunderstanding or the invoice or payment may have gotten lost in the mail. A simple call to the accounts payable contact at the client's company asking, "When might we expect payment?", may be all that is required. In a perverse sort of way I actually enjoyed these situations and the challenge of finding ways to expedite payment.

Summary

I spent a lot of time with clients trying to understand what they were trying to accomplish and finding the most expeditious way of doing it. It was consultive selling at its best and I felt as if I were a doctor asking the client where it hurt. In the course of ten years, we dealt with more than 300 contacts at 100 accounts. I used networking techniques in the markets of which I was familiar and did do some occasional cold calling. This mostly consisted of dropping off my card, explaining to the receptionist what we did, and asking her for names for subsequent follow-up. The driver for most clients to have work done by us was usually related to their need to have a qualification test performed thus enhancing their chance of capturing additional business. I called on engineers and operations personnel in the course of selling our service.

I relied on basic mechanics and design techniques in this job. In many cases, after discussions with the client, I would do a rough sketch showing how we would test his parts and would include drawings of fixtures that we might need to build. We would refine this via internal discussions and then estimate the cost of the required hardware, manpower, and equipment rental. A basic knowledge of hydraulics, strength of materials, statics, and failure analysis was useful in this job.

I learned a lot about a number of pieces of oilfield and mechanical equipment, what they were used for and their limitations. I had a new appreciation for the value of a good network and to not be apprehensive while making cold calls. The business aspects of quoting, forecasting, and cash flow were invaluable lessons to learn.

I enjoyed my years working at H.O. Mohr. Because we were involved in research and testing I was encouraged to maintain a bound logbook of my daily activities including discussions with customers. I have maintained that discipline and it has helped me over the years by documenting details, recording decisions that were made, and serving as a tool for writing reports to management.

4
Manufacturer's Representative

We never lead with product; we lead with need.
                    —Zig Ziglar, sales trainer

As I mentioned in the last chapter, I agreed to work part-time for a manufacturer's representative company named Choctaw Sales. It was a straight commission arrangement, and any costs I incurred were to my own account. Choctaw sold chemicals, various shipping containers, and had several lines of material handling and packaging equipment they represented. They needed a technical person to follow-up on a number of leads they had been given by the manufacturers they represented, commonly called principals. I was attracted to the mechanical equipment more than the containers and chemicals.

Choctaw represented a company who manufactured various bag packers. The fifty- to eighty-pound bags into which various plastics are typically shipped are called valve bags because they have an opening on one side of the paper or plastic bag that has a small cardboard flapper (or valve) in it. When the bag is placed on the spout of the packer, the spout forces the cardboard flapper upward so that the material can be forced into the bag. When it is removed from the spout, the material in the bag causes the cardboard flapper to close. Material can be forced into the bag by either an auger in the packer or by air pushing it in.

The fifty- to eighty-pound bags that are used to contain cement or food products are called open-mouth bags. The top part of the bag is held open with a set of clamping jaws while it is being gravity filled with material from above. Once a preset weight is reached, a damper in the machine closes and the flow stops. The bag is then released and it is either sewn closed or hot glue is applied to seal it.

In both designs, load cells are used to measure the weight and a series of relays causes a mechanism to stop the flow of material at the programmed set point. Either a clamp holding the valve bag onto the spout or the jaws of the open-mouth bag releases it. Both types of bags can utilize a robotic arm to place the bags on the packer and a conveyor can then be used to transport the bag to the next operation once it is packed.

This principal also manufactured machines to load and empty 2,000-pound bulk bags. Lots of products are shipped or stored in these large flexible canvas containers including agricultural produce, plastics, and minerals. Either a slide gate or an iris valve is used to stop the flow of product into a bulk bag once the targeted weight is achieved. To unload one of these bulk bags, optional vibrators, thumpers, or other devices can be specified to enhance flow.

Choctaw also represented companies who built roller conveyors for packed products and pneumatic and aero-mechanical conveyors, elevators, and screw feeders for loose products. Some of their principals manufactured items for the food industry including check weighers, metal detectors, and magnetic traps. To keep loads of fifty-pound bags in place on a pallet, they had lines of stretch wrappers and shrink wrappers.

I was absolutely enthralled with all these machines and made a number of trips to the plants where they were built so I could learn to sell their equipment. However, my very first sale was not a machine but a carton of drum covers. These are plastic covers that snap in place over fifty-five-gallon drums to prevent moisture from getting into the bunghole (or opening) of the drum. I made $35 on that sale and it encouraged me that I could actually sell some of Choctaw's items. I was able to get leads on a number of opportunities for the more expensive capital equipment and quoted some of them. However, I discovered that no matter how hard I tried, this type of sale could take a long time to come to fruition. There were always layers of management that had to approve capital investments and that took time.

I realized that sales could be a lot like farming. I could concentrate my efforts and harvest the fast growing expense items, like drum covers, but I'd never make much money doing it. Or, I could cultivate the slow growing capital expansion projects where the higher commission opportunities were. I decided to take this latter course.

First Big Sale

Leads are fed to a manufacturer's representative company by the principals who in turn receive them from the magazines in which they advertise or from the contacts they've made at trade shows that they attend. Territories are usually exclusive to a given rep company. Invoicing is typically done by the principal who then sends a commission check to the rep agency once the invoice is paid. Sometimes payments took a while. At Choctaw Sales we usually insisted that we do the invoicing to the end-user and when we got paid we sent a check to the manufacturer for the value of the equipment he supplied. This speeds up the time for us to be paid for our services and causes the principal to treat us with more respect since we are really his customer.

I was assigned Dow Chemical in Freeport, Texas, as an account. I met a young engineer there and we started discussing a complex pneumatic conveyor system to transport plastic pellets in his plant. We found a local manufacturer who would work with us on this project and we had several meetings with the engineer and the manufacturer to lay out the design. On the day that the quote was to be sent the manufacturer became insistent that they would build the system only if they did the invoicing and would pay us a 10% commission after they got paid. This was not agreeable to us and I told them so. After much haggling, I got their sales manager to agree to give us a 15% commission in exchange for us agreeing to let them do the invoicing.

During the course of the next three months, we set up and attended several technical meetings about the project in both Houston and Freeport. The system was built, installed, and debugged. The manufacturer was paid but did not send us our commission. After a number of phone calls, we finally got a check for 10%, not the agreed-upon 15%.

While all this was going on, I was getting paid a minimum amount from H.O. Mohr based upon the days I worked for them. I was also using the severance package from Hydril to help fund expenses for the more speculative Choctaw Sales opportunities. Sometimes I'd daydream that my family was in a small plane that was gradually losing altitude and one day we'd crash financially. So, the pneumatic equipment manufacturer's commission of less than the agreed upon amount became a personal issue with me and Pat, the owner of Choctaw Sales. We threatened to sue the manufacturer and he eventually paid us the full amount. I received $6,000 in commissions as well as a hard lesson about verbal agreements. From the time I signed on with Choctaw Sales until I got the full amount of this commission check, about nine months had elapsed. It was a welcome relief and I felt like our mythical little plane had gained a little altitude.

More Projects

After this I sold a large bulk bag packer to Exxon Chemical, several fifty-pound packers to Dow Chemical, and a stretch wrapper to another petrochemical company in the Houston ship channel area. I was starting to really enjoy this work.

I attended a trade show in Chicago dealing with material handling and packaging equipment. While there, I met an engineer who mentioned that he was in charge of a plant expansion in Houston for a metal powder that would be used in VCR tapes. I gave him some information on our principals and we exchanged cards. There is something to be said about the novelty of meeting someone in another city at such an event. The customer tends to remember the occasion and the sales rep. He lived in St. Louis and I tried in vain to contact him for follow-up. On one occasion, his secretary happened to mention that he had gone to Houston. So, that night I called the one big hotel nearest their Houston plant and asked for him. He answered the phone and asked how it was that I knew he was staying there. My simple answer was that it was my business to know such things. Impressed, we met at the Houston plant shortly after that and it led to a fairly large project for our company. I learned that people admire persistence and are flattered when you go the extra mile to make contact with them.

During this time I had all sorts of unusual opportunities present themselves to me. I sold some equipment to a company and they mentioned that they had an old stretch wrap machine for sale. This device has a turntable upon which a pallet loaded with bags, boxes, or other containers is placed. The operator then pulls some of the clear plastic stretch wrap material from off a spindle mounted to a mast and fastens it by jamming it between the packages. By pressing the start button, the table begins rotating as more material is wrapped around the load while the spindle moves up and then down the mast. I told them I'd keep their used machine in mind as

I made calls on other customers.

Not a week later another customer asked me if I knew of any used stretch wrap machines in the area. I described the one I'd been told about and then called the first customer asking what he'd take for it. I marked it up by 25% and quoted that to the second client as a cash deal. He said the price and the terms seemed reasonable. So, I got a pick up truck and had the machine loaded in it and delivered it to the second client. Having visited both companies, I knew they were located fairly closely but I had to take a half-mile circuitous route to get to the second company because of the location of railroad tracks and the way the area was laid out. Only after I got the check in my hand did I realize that the back yards of both companies were adjacent to each other!

On another occasion, one of my good customers called up two days before Christmas and needed to see me immediately. He had to spend $20,000 before the end of the year or his next year's budget would be cut. I visited him and we looked through catalogs for something for him to buy. He settled on some items I'd never sold before. His company sent us a check the next day and the equipment wasn't delivered until three months later. It made for a wonderful Christmas.

Once I had a good customer call me to ask if I could have a tumbler built for his plastic compounding company. They took various pigments, blended them together, and then injected them into a flow stream of hot plastic, which is then extruded into spaghetti-like streams. This is then cooled and the spinning blade of a pelletizer cuts them into pellets. These are then bagged and find use in the manufacture of automobile dashboards and door panels and many other products. Not knowing what a tumbler was, he suggested I come see the one they currently had in their test lab.

It had a trunnion-mounted blending pot that was polished to a mirror finish on the inside. They would put different colored pigment material into the pot, screw on the lid, and then it would rotate for a predetermined time. After this they would do a trial run of the plastic to see if it had the correct color as prescribed by their customer. They only had one of these machines and as I started taking measurements to duplicate it I noticed that there were some Japanese markings on it. I asked my customer about that and he said they'd had it a while, that it came from Japan, and they didn't want to order another one from there because the cost of the equipment and its transportation was too expensive. So, we copied a Japanese machine, which in all likelihood had been a copy of an American one. What a country!

We once sold some liquid filling equipment to a client in Houston. It would receive four fifty-five-gallon drums and would first rotate one until the bunghole or opening of the drum was in a certain position. Then a titanium lance would automatically be inserted into the drum near the bottom and liquid would be injected into it. During the filling the lance would slowly move upward so that the end of it was just below the surface of the fluid. Once filled, the machine would repeat this process for all four drums.

The electronics to do all this was complicated. About two months after we had had this machine installed and debugged, I happened to call the customer to check out how everything was working. He said that it had operated flawlessly until the day before when the machine suddenly shut down and an error message saying "major electrical malfunction" came up on the display. They had called the manufacturer who had them connect a port on the machine to a cable modem and they were able to "debug" it remotely. I contacted the principal and inquired about this. He said, "All our machines are programmed to automatically shut down sixty days after start-up. We then check to see if we've been paid or not." I admired this company's creativity but questioned their integrity and the quality of the rest of their customer base.

Sales Techniques

Pat, the owner of Choctaw Sales, had been in various sales positions during his long career. He was also a good sales trainer. I remember traveling with him in the car while trying to set up appointments on his cell phone. I called the main number of one company and asked to speak to my contact. After the call, Pat asked rather harshly why I didn't state my name and affiliation when asking to speak to my customer. He said that you have to think enough of yourself and respect what you do to not be afraid to announce who you are. In many cases, a person's receptionist will ask who you are anyway but it comes across more professional if you volunteer it before being asked.

I have also found it useful to ask if the person on the other end of the line has a minute to talk. If I don't have his attention because he's distracted with something else, it won't be a fruitful conversation. This can be risky if you've tried many times previously to get him on the phone. However, people appreciate your politeness in asking and it enhances communication.

A Sandler Sales Institute trainer once showed me a technique to use when you need an answer from a contact that will not return a phone call. When you leave a message on his answering machine, you explain why you need his response and that it is okay if the answer is no. It is surprising how many times giving someone permission to give you a negative answer will cause them to return the phone call. I've also learned that when leaving voice mail for someone who knows my phone number, that the polite thing to do is leave the number. It saves them time and the aggravation of looking it up. Thus they are more likely to return the call. I also make it a point to say the numbers slowly and distinctly.

I remember once referring to my presentation on a certain piece of equipment as a "pitch." Pat came unglued. He said that kind of talk is for "rope, dope, and soap salesmen." A pitch sounds too much like a snake oil salesman's harangue while trying to sell his product. We are professionals and we deliver presentations, he explained. I like that a lot better.

Pat was always trying to add to my sales skills and loaned me a number of audio tapes (this was before CDs) by Zig Ziglar, Dennis Waitley, Tommy Hopkins, and many others. Their inspiring messages were delivered with humor that made them easy to listen to and remember. Some of these tapes addressed sales closing techniques and ways of building credibility with your customer.

I remember quoting an elevator to a petrochemical customer. This is a machine that consists of a large continuous rubber belt with rectangular buckets attached to it. It is used to transport dry products vertically from one point to another. This particular application involved raising plastic pellets more than fifty feet straight up in a highly congested area of the plant. I had provided something similar to a biocide company located about three miles away. I had put a number of items in that plant and had always done them a good job. I asked them if I could bring in an engineer from a non-competing company. They allowed me to do so and we got a nice order out of it.

I find that references can be a powerful and professional way to develop business. As long as you are sure that your reference thinks highly of your product or service, it is not always necessary to ask their permission. I have mentioned our continuing business with certain companies and have name-dropped the experts with those companies in conversations with new clients. In most cases they will not check with those references, but even if they did, I'd feel comfortable with the outcome.

A tacit source of continuing business revolves around our proclivity to develop habits. For instance, I've noticed that people who meet periodically sit in the same chairs at each meeting. In my own life, I realized recently that I drive out of my way in order to drop off and pick up my clothes from a particular dry cleaner. There are a number of establishments on my route to and from work. However, the owner of the one I go to is friendly, does a good job, and has a fair price. I'll keep going to him until something changes enough over a threshold amount to warrant the time and effort to find another dry cleaners. When I think of getting my clothes cleaned, I only think of that establishment.

The same holds true in selling technical products or services. There may be some additional hurdles in terms of formal quotes or group decision-making, but people don't generally like to change suppliers if they perceive they are getting a good product or service at a fair price. I had more than one company who always called me first when planning a plant expansion or buying a new piece of equipment. It was as if they didn't realize I had competitors. It was simply too time consuming and difficult to find others to help them with their needs. If you are passionate about doing a customer a good job, they will return the favor by being loyal to you.

Engineering and Construction Companies

The local chapter of the American Society of Mechanical Engineers formed a material handling technical subchapter of which I was a founding member. We brought in some of our principals to address the group at meetings and participated in a local trade show in which we displayed our equipment. Through these efforts I got to meet a lot of people employed by engineering and construction (E&C) companies.

I began to specialize in large projects for which an E&C company was employed to organize the work. This was rewarding both professionally and financially because I would frequently get in on the ground floor and help educate the E&C engineers about my equipment and therefore help write the specifications. We would quote on the parts of these projects with which we were familiar. Typically, that section of the engineering bid dealing with the scope of work was the easiest to understand and comply with. The parts of the request for quote (RFQ) describing the terms and conditions, warranties, packaging, safety considerations, and many other issues were problematic. I would go through all these sections and highlight those paragraphs and clauses that were of concern and alert our principals about them. The liability mostly fell on them and they appreciated my helping them work through these issues.

Sometimes we got pressure from both our principals and clients. One of the firms we represented always demanded a 20% deposit before accepting any order. We had worked together on a quote for a particular E&C company whose representative had warned me beforehand that they would not pay the required prepayment. My principal encouraged me with certain arguments that always worked and suggested that I use them to convince the E&C company to pay it. I made an appointment to drop off the bid to the E&C representative and to talk with him about it. As I walked in his office, his first words were, "If you're here to talk about the 20% down payment, we have nothing to discuss." I handed him our quote, smiled and said, "You're right; goodbye," then shook his hand and walked out. The look on his face was worth the risk of losing the business. I immediately called the principal and explained to him what had happened. The client also called him, the manufacturer blinked and allowed him to waive the prepayment. The principal handled most of the technical and commercial issues on this project and we were paid a nice commission on a timely basis.

Not all these projects went smoothly. There was one in which the E&C company was located in Houston, one of our principals had a manufacturing plant in Houston, and another principal and the plant in which the equipment was to be installed were in New Jersey. We had been warned by another manufacturer's rep agency that this E&C company was hard to do business with. Nevertheless, the project was of sufficient size that we were tempted to quote on it. The E&C company demanded a performance bond and required that we deliver the equipment to the site. Nearly all other projects are quoted on a free on-board (FOB) basis in which the manufacturer agrees to load it on a truck and then the customer legally takes delivery of it at that time.

We got the purchase order to provide a number of flexible screw feeders that would dump material into hoppers that we would have custom-made in Houston. There is always a challenge and a risk when providing a machine that must interface with another piece of equipment. Our principals provided layout drawings of what this customized machinery would look like. The New Jersey principal's drawings were rather unusual, showing cables supporting long cantilevered spouts in which the feed augers turned. The client insisted, and I agreed, that a more robust support mechanism was needed. About that time the principal's engineer who had worked on this system in New Jersey left the company. The client was getting nervous because of the delays in getting drawings made and approved. We finally received them and the customer approved them. However, after a few weeks he realized he was not reading these drawings correctly and the machines, when finally installed, would need to be turned around 180 degrees. That would not normally be a problem, but the highly congested area in which this equipment would be placed necessitated that the support legs be redesigned to not interfere with an adjacent machine. I spent a great deal of time sending faxes and making phone calls to solve problems and keep the project on schedule.

The design of some custom-built stainless steel hoppers in Houston went smoothly. I proofed all the drawings before giving them to my client and was able to catch some errors before he saw them. The interior walls of the hoppers were polished to a 220-grit finish, which means that 220-grit sandpaper is used in the polishing process. After they were built, we had a plant visit and the customer approved the hoppers. The most troublesome part of this aspect of the project had to do with the transportation issue. We had agreed to include the trucking price in the quote. We initially contemplated renting a trailer and delivering them ourselves. However, when we looked at the time, cost, and logistical issues involved in that we started calling trucking companies.

We were surprised at the variance in quotes between firms. It was a time of decontrol in which trucking companies' rates were no longer dictated by the federal government. We were able to find a reputable company whose quote was quite a bit lower than the rate we had assumed in our original bid. However, because one of the hoppers was especially tall, it was imperative that the trucker know the proper route to take so as not to run into the bottom side of an overpass. We carefully loaded the hoppers on a truck one day and I spent two sleepless nights hoping that they made it there without damage.

Fortunately, the equipment got there without a problem. The New Jersey-based principal agreed to use his own company trucks and transport his feeders to the site. He did so but when the items got there, the client insisted that their engineer be present when they were put in place. This is not normally done but the principal's owner graciously agreed to do so. About three weeks later, they tried to start the feeders but one of them made a loud banging noise. The principal had not turned his equipment on at the shop to test it and discovered an auger flight was hitting the inside of its internal hopper. He agreed to take it back and realign it.

As you can imagine, we earned our money on this project. I spent an inordinate amount of time trying to soothe the situation and keep it moving forward. It was not a pleasant experience being pressured by the client and the principal. It was a happy day when we finally received the last payment for the "project from hell," as we humorously called it.

Being Organized Pays Off

In many sales engineering functions the natural talent of an engineer to be organized and maintain records can be helpful. In the project described above I kept copious notes of conversations, cost estimates, dimensional changes, and time schedules. This helped save us a lot of hassle when the customer started changing things.

We were once approached by a chemical company to build some screw feeders that were to be placed outside of a high temperature plastic pellet dryer. Because of the corrosive nature of the liquids that the pellets had been exposed to, all contact surfaces of the feeder—housing, auger, and supports—had to be constructed of an expensive duplex stainless steel. In addition, the specification called for a 400-grit finish on all these surfaces. Because the pellets needed to be cooled, the housing had to be surrounded by a water jacket.

We bid on this with the help of a Texas-based manufacturer and promptly were awarded a contract to build five of them. Because of a misunderstanding, the principal did not realize that the cooling jacket had to be ASME certified as a pressure vessel. In addition, due to the hardness of the duplex stainless steel, they were having a hard time meeting the 400-grit specification. We were able to assist them by employing a company in Houston to polish the surfaces and another company to build the coded pressure vessel. There were some cost overruns on the project but because of the timeliness of my client's requirements they paid extra to have these things done promptly.

I maintained a large file on all the twists and turns during the six month fabrication of these five units. They were installed, we were paid, and I heard nothing more from my client. About three years later, I got a call from an engineer with the chemical company. The person I had dealt with had left the company and they could not find any of the drawings we'd sent up there with the equipment. They needed two more of these machines and wondered if we could quote them the cost of building them.

I knew exactly where to find the file in my attic where I'd stored it. We were able to quote these machines, get the purchase order, and have them fabricated in three months. My job mostly consisted of keeping the files straight and making a couple of trips to the manufacturer. I later calculated how much money I made in commissions and it worked out to more than $300 per hour! Being organized had paid off handsomely.

Later in my career, I worked for a company that subscribed to the Japanese notion of 5S. In English, this stands for sort, systemize, scrub, standardize, and sustain. When this was first introduced at the company, many parts of the facility that did not look presentable were cleaned up and organized in such a way as to improve efficiency. Because we as humans use the halo effect without even realizing it, we assume that if a place looks good, it probably employs quality people and produces quality products and services. It was relatively easy for me to adopt this philosophy as I have found it to be useful in running my office and home files. I clean off my desk every evening, thus avoiding the depression of walking into a disorderly office the next day.

Another aspect of being organized has to do with time management. I used to make a daily to-do list. In Stephen R. Covey's book *The Seven Habits of Highly Effective People* this subject is addressed. He recommends planning by the week instead of by the day. This has the effect of empowering you, as you plan your week, of listing those things that really need to be done. In addition, by categorizing them into groups such as family time, spiritual goals, business tasks, etc, you can become even more in control of what is important. Finally, this relieves the anxiety you might feel when something unexpected comes up or someone comes in your office and talks incessantly about an unimportant issue. You know that you have all week to get the things done on that list and somehow most of them get done.

Summary

I found this work challenging both technically and commercially. As I mentioned earlier, it was a little like farming. You could be the best salesperson in the world, but in this market, it took time to grow the opportunities. I did some cold calling but my most productive selling was the result of networking professionally through the ASME and by following up on leads generated by our principals. I dealt with more than 80 companies and 200 contacts during the more than ten years I did this work on a part-time basis.

I was fascinated with all the various machines used in the petrochemical and food industries and enjoyed large projects with many machines interfacing with one another. The technical skills I used during this part of my career consisted of mechanics, materials, design, and some failure analysis. I spent a great deal of time and energy communicating between clients and principals and delivered information accurately using drawings, letters, and verbal conversations.

During this time I learned a lot about a number of machines that are used in material and packaging applications. I came to appreciate the importance of references, the fact that customer habits can lead to customer loyalty, and some important things about communications, including phone etiquette. The need to maintain organized files was also confirmed to me.

5
Short-Term Consulting

In the middle of difficulty lies opportunity.
—Albert Einstein

As mentioned previously, my arrangements with H.O. Mohr and Choctaw Sales were such that I could literally wake up each morning and decide which opportunity to pursue that day. H.O. Mohr's business was steady and they paid me based upon the days I worked plus a small end-of-the year bonus depending upon the company's profitability. They reimbursed me for customer entertainment but because I was a contractor they offered no benefits such as medical insurance, holidays, or vacation. Choctaw's remuneration was solely based upon earned commissions and any travel expenses or entertainment costs were to my account.

We were successful at Mohr in attracting a lot of mechanical testing for qualification purposes. Even though the oil industry was not doing well, the service companies were using this time to develop new products and therefore qualification testing was imperative. The most profitable activity for us involved testing tubing and casing connections and we were good at it. We helped develop testing methods and equipment that became industry standards. One downside to this part of the business had to do with the preparation, transportation, and handling of these highly engineered samples. At one point, I had sold quite a bit of these tests but our clients were taking a long time getting them to us. The samples for one big project were damaged in transit and I could tell that we were going to have a cash flow problem.

Pulsation Dampeners

One day I approached my former boss at Hydril and asked him if he knew anyone who needed a sales engineer to work for them for one day a week. He thought for a minute, smiled, and said he did. In fact, he knew someone who needed a sales engineer for a brief period to make sales calls, promoting a technical product, two days a week. It was him. He said Hydril was looking for someone to promote their line of industrial pulsation dampeners to the petrochemical companies in the Texas area. They had sales people, but they were unfamiliar with that market, had no contacts in it, and were unsure about the safety training that would be required to enter the gates of these companies.

I was knowledgeable about this equipment, having worked with the engineer who had taken Hydril's oilfield design and modified it for less severe applications in industrial environments. A pulsation dampener, or PD, reduces the strain on piping and valves by minimizing the pressure waves that occur when a fluid is being pumped by a piston type pump. Hydril's design consisted of a spherical shaped housing, a rubber bladder available in several different compounds, and a head having an inlet and an outlet. An adjustable amount of pressure from air or nitrogen is applied to the backside of the bladder through a port. PDs are useful in extending the life of piping and preventing leaks in flanges.

He asked if I was interested and wanted to know how much money I needed to do this work. I did some quick math in my head and bumped the daily fee I charged H. O. Mohr by 20%. He said that sounded fine to him and we shook hands on it. I grabbed some literature on the way out the door, telling him I'd call him in a few days after I read up on this equipment.

High Pressure Flanges

The next day I had lunch with a friend of mine who worked at a company called Taper-Lok. During the meal, I happened to mention to him, in confidence, what had happened the day before. He asked some questions about how I planned on doing this and what contacts I had in the petrochemical industry. Then he mentioned that his management might also be interested in this type of arrangement. His boss called me the next day and wanted to get together soon to discuss this. We met shortly after this and he said they had a line of high pressure, specialty flanges for use in the oil industry that they thought might have application in the petrochemical business. He wanted to know if I might consider promoting this product on a short-term, trial basis. When I answered in the affirmative, he wanted to know what I would charge. I took the amount I had quoted to Hydril and increased it by 20%. He said that if I would invoice them every two weeks that would be fine. We shook hands on it and I grabbed a bunch of literature on the way out the door, telling him I'd call him in a few days after I read up on this equipment. I began to wonder if there was no upper limit on how much I could charge.

Shortly after that, Harvey Mohr mentioned to me that they might have to cut back on the number of days I worked for them. I said, "No problem." I spent several days reading up on PDs and on Taper-Lok's line of specialty flanges. I touched base with both companies and then began calling engineers I knew to show them these products. I would bring samples and literature and try to find applications for these products. I'd also ask for references of others I could call on. At the end of each week, I'd send a report to each company on the contacts I'd made and what opportunities I uncovered.

After three months of effort, Hydril decided to not renew this arrangement. I had made calls for them for the equivalent of twenty-four days but was not able to sell any of their PDs. So, I contacted a friend who was the president of a company named Nordstrom Valves who manufactured tapered plug valves.

Plug Valves

These simple devices consist of a body with an inlet and outlet and a tapered plug with a slot in it. By turning the valve ninety degrees the flow of fluid through the valve can be turned off and on. A shroud or bonnet on top prevents the tapered plug from blowing out and has an adjustment to drive the plug downward into the mating surfaces. Lubricant can be injected into this area to help seal the valve and prevent flow-by past the closed taper. My friend was not interested at first but had the sales manager contact me to discuss this in further detail. We had breakfast and he mentioned that the company was concerned about small gas emissions from their equipment and had developed a secondary bonnet that could be used to capture any errant gas. He wanted to know if I'd be interested in promoting the valve and especially with that option. I answered in the affirmative and then he wanted to know how much I charged. I took the amount I'd quoted Taper-Lok and bumped it another 20%. He said that would be fine and wanted to know when I could go to one of their Houston distributors for training. Shortly after that I spent a day in training and then began to promote their valve.

During the fourth week of this campaign, I was calling on a customer who said he needed two of these valves for his tank farm. This is an ideal application as the fluid being controlled is a liquid and the valve can stay in a certain position—opened or closed—for an extended period. I called up one of Nordstrom's distributors and they provided the valves. Not bad for only making calls for them for four days. I scouted out some other opportunities for Nordstrom but was only able to sell a couple more valves and after about four months we ended the agreement.

However, the Taper-Lok management wanted more of my time so I worked for them two to three days a week for more than a year. I would make calls on my existing contacts and show them literature and a sample flange.

During this time I also worked about a day a week for H.O. Mohr. There was a metallurgist affiliated with H.O. Mohr who asked me to promote his services a half-day per week. My first call on his behalf resulted in a nice project for him. This type of consulting can be rather stressful because I began to expand my customer base which required a lot of phone calls to set up appointments. My goal was to make at least three face-to-face calls per day. Since I was paid based upon my ability to see people, holidays were particularly bad. Who wants to see a salesman when there is a Christmas party to go to?

Taper-Lok had not promoted their flanges to any E&C companies so I began to set up presentations with a number of Houston-based companies. We'd offer them lunch and give a talk about the flanges. I also attended a two-day trade show and was able to get a lot of traffic in the booth by talking to the engineers as they walked by. Unfortunately, after more than a year's effort I was not able to sell one of their flanges. Part of the problem was pricing. They had a good design but there were other, less expensive solutions. The other problem was the lack of applications. Most surface installations in the oilfield involve processes characterized by high pressures but temperatures that are not extreme. The downstream industry in which I was attempting to sell Taper-Lok's equipment has the opposite situation and therefore there didn't seem to be many applications for what they were offering. So, we mutually decided to terminate the relationship. About this time, Harvey Mohr asked if I had more time to spend with his company and I consented to do so.

Stereolithography

Harvey got intrigued with a technology that allows 3-D reproduction in plastic from engineering drawings. It is a rapid prototyping technique called stereolithography and involves the curing of a plastic bath when a laser hits it. Once a layer is cured, the base upon which the 3-D replica will emerge moves down into the fluid and the next layer is solidified. At the end of the process, the base is raised to reveal a finished product. This technology has found use in the medical arts in designing customized prosthetic devices and has even been utilized to duplicate (through a CT or MRI scan) what a patient's brain looks like so a surgeon can determine the best operating procedure to employ. For industrial applications, this process can be used to make a solid replica of a finished part to get a quick feel for what it looks like. The replica can also be used to make a mold so production parts can be cast.

H.O. Mohr bought a couple of machines and it was fascinating to watch parts being made in this way. The machines were programmed during the day and were turned on as we left for the evening. In the morning the completed parts would be sitting above the liquid plastic awaiting separation from the elevator and finish sanding. In addition to my other duties, I was asked to scout out potential opportunities for stereolithography in the oil industry. I discovered that the manufacturers of certain types of drill bits mold the base out of metal. Most oil-field drill bits consist of a base with a threaded pin facing up which is screwed into the bottom of the drill pipe. A typical bit has three cones that rotate against the formation as the drill pipe is turned. These cones have hardened teeth on them that impact the formation as they rotate around and cause the rocks to chip off. A fluid called mud is pumped down the drill pipe through the bit and impacts these chips through nozzles at the bottom of the bit. Because the mud is thick and flowing quickly, the chips are forced up the annular space outside the drill pipe where they are disposed of on the surface.

Another type of bit consists of a number of man-made cylindrical diamonds, which are mounted into the drill bit base. As the bit turns the diamonds scrape away the rock formation and the chips are disposed of as described above. There are numerous designs for the base in that the quantity, location, and angles at which the diamonds are held can vary by manufacturer and the type of formation being drilled. New designs are continually being introduced. I presented the advantages of using stereolithography to several diamond drill bit manufacturers and was able to get a few orders.

However, for a variety of reasons, H.O. Mohr was not successful in this venture and it had a deleterious effect on cash flow, operations, and morale. Something was in the air, and one morning it was announced that the company was to be sold to another company. They called six of us involved in the operation of the company into a meeting to discuss the transition. I looked around and realized that of the group, I was the only one not an employee and that I had been there the longest. I could provide quotes for projects as large as $300,000 on my authority (but naturally always had another set of eyes look at them before submission). The company had treated me well and we had had a lot of fun but I sensed that I should start looking around for another opportunity. (My wife had been saying that it was time to grow up and get a real job like everybody else.)

Fortunately for me, I had recently seen an ad in the local newsletter of a professional society of which I was a member. A recruiter was looking for an engineer who was familiar with oilfield operations and various industry standards to help launch new products into the oil industry. I called him and discussed the opportunity with him.

Summary

This part of my sales career was a lot like being a scout. I went looking for opportunities, would report on them and someone else would get the purchase order. I did a lot of prospecting, cold calling, and spent a lot of time on the phone trying to set up sales calls. The technical skills I employed included mechanics and materials. I derived pleasure (and compensation) from showing the companies I represented where they might sell their products.

I found that a technical sales rep carries certain assets with him that can help him uncover sales opportunities. For instance, the natural optimism of a salesperson coupled with the passion and curiosity of technical things can allow you to find customers for the products that you represent. It helped me discover alternate uses for existing products, like employing stereolithography to the making of drill bit molds or attempting to sell oilfield PDs into industrial applications or high pressure flanges into process industries.

Unlike other corporate functions a sales rep brings with him a valuable asset—his customer base. Like one man told me his father always told him, "Son, if you can weld, you can always get a job." Likewise, the skills and reputation of a good technical salesperson will always be in demand. There is a need for people who can explain technical things in a non-technical manner.

I learned a lot about persistence and that there are lucrative opportunities for representing companies on a short-term basis. You just have to use your entrepreneurial talents to uncover them.

6

A New Material for an Old Industry

Engineering is the conscious application of science to the problems of economic production.
—H. P. Gillette, engineer & publisher

I met with the recruiter who had placed the ad in the ASM International newsletter and he seemed encouraged that I might be the candidate that this mystery company was seeking. He did say that at one time the company had had two sales people in Houston but the position had been vacant for about six months. He also mentioned that the opportunity had to do with introducing a specialty metal into the oilfield.

We eventually set up an interview with the vice president of sales of this company. Their name was RMI Titanium and they produced specialty items made of a number of grades of titanium. During the interview, I discovered that they had sold some parts for use in downhole safety valves as well as for sample bottles to obtain virgin samples of hydrocarbons while still in the well. They had manufactured large diameter titanium pipe for use in highly corrosive geothermal wells and for use in certain underwater applications. I was intrigued because I had some knowledge of metallurgy from my college courses and had heard of some of the marvelous properties of titanium alloys. I agreed to go to their plant in Ohio to see how the product is manufactured.

All About Titanium

The trip was very informative. They receive the titanium as relatively pure nuggets. They take a certain weight of them, add in aluminum, vanadium, and other elements, and then pour the contents into a mixer. This is all pressed together at room temperature into the shape of a large brick. From a distance, it looks like a giant sponge and so that is what it is called. A large number of sponges are temporarily placed adjacent to each other on an angle iron frame and welded together in an oxygen-free environment. Eventually, this welded mass of titanium sponge is lifted up and suspended inside a water-jacketed melt chamber. It is held just above the bottom of the vessel and high voltage is applied to it and the melt chamber. The generated electrical arc melts the titanium. When this process is completed and the titanium is cooled, the bottom of the vessel is removed and the titanium billet is extracted. It can be as large as 3′ in diameter and 6′ or 7′ long. It is eventually heated up again and forged into smaller, more manageably-sized billets. From there, the billets can be used in an extrusion press or a rotary piercer to produce seamless pipe.

Titanium started being used in aircraft applications in the 1940s. It has the highest ratio of strength to density of any known industrial metal. Pure titanium, referred to as Grade 1, has a yield strength of 25,000 psi. By varying the amount of trace elements in a titanium matrix, engineers discovered that they could achieve 40,000 psi yield strength. These are known as Grades 2, 3 & 4 and find very few applications. Sometime in the late 1940s, it was discovered that by adding 6% aluminum and 4% vanadium, yields of 120,000 psi could be obtained (most carbon steel used in construction applications is rated at 36,000 psi yield). Although titanium makes up less than 1% of the earth's crust, it is the ninth most common element and the seventh most common metal. It is particularly hard to process because of its affinity for oxygen. You cannot heat up a batch of titanium in an open-hearth furnace, like you can with iron ore. It would grab the oxygen out of the air and you'd end up with various titanium oxides. A chemical process is used to go from titanium ore sand to the nuggets I saw in my plant visit. The most common ore from which titanium is refined is called ilmenite, $FeTiO_3$, which is found in Western Australia, the Ukraine, New Zealand, Canada, and Norway. Another ore is called rutile, principally TiO_2, which is found in many places in the world, including North America.

After titanium pipe is produced it has to be pickled in a mixture of hydrofluoric and nitric acid or mechanically ground to remove a thin, crack-initiating layer called alpha case. For these reasons, it is expensive to produce and form into useful products.

However, there are certain applications for which a titanium alloy can be an elegant and cost-effective solution. It has great corrosion resistance and a low Young's modulus (a measure of its stiffness). While this index for steel is 30 million psi, most titanium alloys have a Young's modulus of 18 million psi. It has found use in the bottom and top terminations of underwater risers in the oil industry because of its corrosion resistance and lower stiffness compared to steel. RMI needed someone to uncover more applications for this product as well as its possible use as tubing in corrosive production wells and as drill pipe.

I waited for several weeks to hear from them after the plant trip. They told me that there was another candidate that they had been talking to and were trying to get him to visit their facility. One day, a friend of mine called to tell me that he was that person and that he was not interested in pursuing the position with RMI. Knowing this greatly enhanced my negotiating position, and the company offered me a job.

On the first workday of January, 1997, I showed up at the executive suite the company had been renting. I began to work through five stacks of files each two-feet tall consisting of unanswered correspondence, phone messages, and other documents.

Titanium Tubing

Once I went through all that paperwork, I started calling my drilling and completion engineering contacts. I presented our case for the use of titanium tubing in corrosive oil and gas wells to technical personnel in a number of companies. One longtime acquaintance at a major oil company agreed to help me determine the feasibility of its use by giving me their tubing string design. The operating conditions included a bottom hole temperature of 420°F with significant amounts of H_2S, a poisonous gas that causes intergranular attack in steel pipe. This company had been using various nickel-chrome-molybdenum grades with good effect. Interestingly, the hotter the service the less corrosion they noticed so they used three different alloys in their wells with the most expensive metallurgy on top. The pipe they were using had a yield of 130,000 psi at room temperature.

Although there were more than twenty-nine recognized grades of titanium at the time, I decided to approach this problem with the use of Grade 5. This is the most common and least expensive material and had been used in the past to make seamless pipe. In my design, I had to thicken up the wall thickness to make allowance for the reduced strength of the titanium. All metals experience a reduction in strength as the temperature increases. When I started applying the empirically derived equations for both nickel-chrome-molybdenum (Ni-Cr-Mo) and Grade 5 titanium, I noticed that, at higher temperatures, titanium's yield strength was lower than Ni-Cr-Mo alloys. The effect of this was that the wall thickness of the titanium had to be increased. When I started trying to calculate prices, I determined that we were less costly than the most expensive nickel-chrome-molybdenum alloy, about tied with the medium service alloy and more expensive than the least critical service alloy. The savings on tubing costs in a $10 million well worked out to about $200,000.

My customer looked at that and said that the savings

would have to be much more than that to justify the necessary qualification tests and the increased risk of using titanium. I asked him what savings figure would allow them to move forward. He replied that if they could save $2 million per well, then it would be worth it. I used that number and worked backwards to determine what the price per pound of the finished pipe would have to be. It was less than our manufacturing cost. I put all this information in a seven-page white paper and sent it to my boss. He was not especially happy with the conclusions but this allowed me time to focus on other, more feasible, oilfield applications.

Titanium Tapered Stress Joints

A subsea riser is used to transport hydrocarbons from an offshore well to the surface. It usually consists of an inner pipe and a protective outer pipe. These can be top tension risers (TTRs) where the pipe is put in tension by attaching it to floating air cans near the ocean surface or by using large hydraulic cylinders. Another type of riser is called a steel catenary riser (SCR) where the bottom termination is horizontal and the top vertically sets into a receptacle on the side of an offshore platform. The bottom of a TTR and the top of an SCR are stress points. As you can imagine, wave motion, currents, wind and occasional movement of a floating platform off station can cause a lot of stress on the riser. Another concern is the fatigue life of a riser due to the above movements and that caused by a phenomenon called vortex induced vibration (VIV). This is the action we see on a stop sign in a high wind. The unstable nature of the flow on one edge of the sign causes it to experience a different pressure than on the other. This causes it to move either forward or backward which makes the other side move the other way. This movement causes the generation of eddy currents first on one side and then the other. The frequency of the vibration is a function of the velocity of the flowing medium and the size of the object on which it is impinging.

Engineers discovered long ago that materials have a fatigue life that is inversely proportional to the induced stress. For instance, if we bend a thin sheet of metal back and forth we will cause it to eventually tear. The further we bend it the sooner it breaks. This can be displayed graphically on an S-N curve, which plots stress (S) on the ordinate and number of cycles (N) on the abscissa. The relationship is not linear. A slight reduction in the applied stress means that the given material can withstand many more cycles.

Because titanium has a lower Young's modulus than steel, it experiences less stress for a given displacement. This means that its fatigue life is many times that of steel. Because of this, it is an excellent material for use as the termination of a subsea riser. The induced stresses caused by the transition between a stiff steel riser and a fixed point can be reduced by having the outside diameter (OD) of the stress joint tapered. It is flanged to the riser at one end and thus has the same OD at that point but has a smaller OD at the other end. Finally, the smoothness of a metal enhances its fatigue life. For this reason, a titanium tapered stress joint (TSJ) is highly polished.

While in an electrolyte like seawater, the nobility of

titanium can cause other metals to which it is electrically attached to corrode. A common way of circumventing this problem is to sleeve the flange holes with a plastic tube and to place ceramic washers under the nuts on the flange studs, thus electrically isolating it. A titanium tapered stress joint is typically coated in rubber to prevent its contact with seawater. The forging, machining, flange welding, polishing, rubber coating, and preparation of a titanium TSJ is an expensive proposition. However, in many cases it is the only solution.

When I first got involved in the marketing of this product, there were perhaps a dozen of these units in service. I knew I'd have to find who the engineers were who were involved in specifying these items in this very specialized technical field. I heard about a Joint Industry Project (JIP) that was being presented to study risers and I attended an introductory meeting to hear what was being proposed. I didn't know a soul, but I received a list of attendees along with their company affiliation. It didn't look like we had an interest in participating in the issue the JIP was addressing but I later began to use the list of contacts to present our credentials about titanium TSJs. My company had in some way been involved in all the applications up to that point and I used that fact to generate interest.

Later on I attended a technical seminar in which nearly all the gurus in this field had gathered to discuss a number of technical issues. When the session was opened for questions, I inquired if anyone knew how many SCRs were in use. The responses from the attendees were that there were anywhere from ten to forty units. No one had ever bothered to list them. Since no one seemed to know, I developed a spreadsheet showing a number of key factors about the ones of which I was aware. This included diameter, water depth, date of installation, location, oil company, etc. My list came to fifteen risers and I sent this to all the gurus I knew and asked them to amend my list or make corrections. Since this spreadsheet was emailed to a number of individuals and I became the keeper of the information, my name and my company's name became recognized in this field. We were invited to participate in a number of JIPs and my ability to set up visits accompanied by our technical personnel was enhanced. Whenever we heard about a new project, I would marshal our materials experts, marine architects, manufacturing personnel, and project management people and we'd discuss details with potential clients. Our involvement was initially confined to the titanium TSJ.

In the course of time our company wanted to get more involved in the actual riser fabrication and acquired a small Houston-based company whose expertise was the welding on of flanges to steel TTRs. Their customer base consisted of a few companies who would turnkey the riser design and used this small company as one vendor out of many. The owners had college degrees in welding technology and were creative in their approaches to methods of insuring proper alignment of the mated parts and in pre- and post-heating of the parts to be welded. They also became interested in a connection that could be welded onto the pipe and would allow the various sections of a TTR to be screwed together. After the acquisition, they stayed with the company to run it and were able to secure a license to manufacture this connection. I helped them develop the literature to promote our new line of riser connectors.

Titanium Drill Pipe

Another possible use for titanium was oilfield drill pipe. Unlike tubing and casing, drill pipe is designed to take variable torque loads because its application is not static but dynamic. The pipe can be anywhere from 2⅜" to 5⅞" in diameter and is upset on the ends. This is a process in which the pipe is heated until it is red hot and an impact load is applied to the end of the pipe. It becomes shorter but thicker on the ends. A heavy screwed connection called a tool joint is then welded to each end of the steel drill pipe. One tool joint has a male connection, called a pin, and the other a female connection, called the box.

Most drilling rigs provide rotary motion at the surface and the entire drill string rotates. This is done by means of a four- or six-sided section of pipe called a kelly which is screwed into the uppermost tool joint. The kelly is run inside a similarly shaped hole in a large flat metal plate called the rotary table that is turned by a geared motor. The kelly can slide vertically as the drill pipe slowly drills a deeper hole.

Many drilling operations nowadays also involve the use of a downhole mud motor to provide rotary motion. The flow of the mud as it is going down the drill pipe is directed through this motor, which is located near the bit. A short section of pipe called a bent sub is screwed into the assembly and is located between the mud motor and the drill bit. As the mud motor turns, the path of the drill bit follows the angle of the bent sub and an arc is generated. During this operation, the drill string slides down the hole. In order to drill straight ahead the drill pipe is slowly rotated as the mud motor is also turning. By this process a horizontal hole can be drilled 4,000 or more feet into a pay zone of interest. This technique has revolutionized the drilling of wells in this country and has dramatically increased the number of producing wells.

One company offered a rental tool that required that the drill pipe rotate while drilling through the arc. They initially tried it with steel pipe and discovered that the pipe failed very quickly because of the fatigue it experienced as the outside of the pipe went from compression to tension as it was being rotated through the arc. They tried fiberglass pipe but it was not rugged enough. Somehow we made contact and explored the possibility of using titanium pipe because of its low Young's modulus. There were several technical problems to be overcome including the need to upset the pipe and somehow to provide a tool joint. Titanium is gall prone and is not a good candidate material for repeat make-and-break applications like drill pipe. So, it was decided to partner with a company who made steel tool joints and to screw them onto the ends of the upset titanium pipe. The idea was to have the repeat make and break action take place on the steel threads and not the titanium. There are certain situations downhole that might cause the titanium pipe to become unscrewed from the steel tool joint. To prevent this, it was decided that there should be diametrical interference between the steel tool joint and the titanium pipe. This involved heating up the steel tool joint so that it grew diametrically. The titanium pipe was then screwed into it and then both were cooled to room temperature.

So, one fine day I found myself straddling a thirty-foot-long piece of titanium pipe while standing on the ways of a large lathe. The tool joint was mounted into its chuck. There was a leather brake wrapped around the far end of the titanium pipe that would provide resistance from it rotating but would allow axial movement. We used induction coils to heat the tool joint to the proper temperature and then turned on the chuck. I then stuck the threaded end of pipe into the female end of the tool joint until the threads started to make up. Once the pin end bottomed out and the brake started screeching, we immediately turned off the lathe and quickly cooled the steel tool joint. We made up eighteen joints and sent them to the field.

It was my pleasure to be present on June 20, 1999, on a rig in Greeley County, Kansas, for the first time that titanium drill pipe went below the rotary. I stayed up a good part of the night recording rate of penetration and RPM as we drilled a curve with several joints of this pipe. We were anxious to know how the pipe held up in this environment and were especially concerned about wear caused by hard rock in the formation. We had measured OD at several points along the length of the pipe and I was not able to detect any noticeable change.

Eventually, a number of wells were successfully drilled with this pipe and we decided to write a couple of technical articles about this process. "Titanium drill pipe a viable option for short-radius horizontal drilling" appeared in the January/February 2000 edition of Drilling Contractor. "Titanium Pipe Proving Ideal for Short-Radius Drilling" was the cover story in the September 2000 edition of the American Oil & Gas Reporter. My contribution was an analysis of the expected fatigue life of the titanium pipe and a comparison to that of steel.

The application of this technology seems limited to shallow wells. Titanium pipe for short-radius drilling was not the success that we hoped it would be.

We also explored its use in very deep vertical wells. The extreme weight of a 30,000´ to 40,000´ string of drill pipe limits the number of drilling rigs that can handle it. However, the high cost of titanium mediates against its use for very deep wells. We investigated the benefits of titanium pipe in extended reach wells. In certain offshore areas of the world such as the North Slope of Alaska or off the UK coast, it is advantageous to drill onshore to hit a pay zone under the seabed many miles away. It was thought that the friction caused by the high weight of steel pipe laying on the low side of the borehole would result in very low torque being available to the drill bit as the pipe was rotated at the surface. However, the increased use of downhole mud motors and even centralizers that serve as bearings along the length of the drill string may have satisfied these concerns.

Other Applications

My job was to find other markets for the company's products and I was constantly looking for niche applications. There was an article in our local paper about a company who retrofitted SUVs to make them resistant to attack by terrorists. They put ballistic grade steel in the vehicles' door panels to prevent bomb fragments and bullets from penetrating. Titanium plate has found use in armor, especially tanks, as a retrofitted sacrificial material due to its flexibility. I met with the owner of the company to see if titanium would help him. One of the problems he faced was that the increased weight of the ballistic grade steel made the vehicles heavier so he had to retrofit them with larger suspension systems. Brake life was also shortened. He became interested in how the lighter weight of titanium might solve his problems. Unfortunately, his interest waned when we started looking at the relative costs of titanium sheet material versus the ballistic grade steel. Well, I tried.

Summary

I enjoyed learning about titanium and appreciated the challenge of presenting it as a possible answer into several different market segments. We were successful in its use in underwater applications as elements of a riser. I like to tell people that I was responsible for selling 60% of the world's titanium tapered stress joints. That sounds impressive until they realize that that represents only twelve units! The financial incentive to use titanium as tubing in corrosive oilfield applications was not there several years ago but because of the increased cost of nickel-chrome-molybdenum alloys, some companies are taking another look at this application. Titanium drill pipe for short-radius applications is a very specialized niche that may not ever develop. Its use in extended reach and very deep vertical wells is limited because of its cost.

I learned that there are ways to quickly establish a presence in new markets. I did this by attending JIP meetings and gathering names of influential people in those areas and by establishing a user group in the case of the riser engineers. I found the work to be a lot like a doctor, finding what the pain was that my potential client was experiencing and trying to determine how my product might best be able to help him.

From a sales standpoint, I learned that persistence in following leads and curiosity about how to help people was important. In addition, it was necessary to be bold in stepping into new markets of which I was unfamiliar.

Technically, I utilized my knowledge of strength of materials, mechanics, design, metallurgy, and failure analysis. The things I learned in various labs in school about taking notes, making measurements and recording data was useful. A broad knowledge about the technical aspects of various oilfield operations was helpful. It was especially gratifying to have coauthored a couple of technical articles about titanium and it helped set us apart as being knowledgeable.

7

Changing Jobs Again

If you aren't fired with enthusiasm, you will be fired with enthusiasm.

—Vince Lombardi

An acquaintance of mine called me one day and wanted me to meet him for breakfast at a nearby restaurant. He was rather elusive about what we would talk about. When we finally met, had a nice meal and a second cup of coffee, he said that his company was trying to upgrade their sales force and wanted me to consider working for him. They competed with a former company that he and I both had worked for, Hydril. I was flattered by his suggestion but I was having a lot of fun finding markets for titanium products. I told him I'd think about it.

He called about a week later wanting to discuss it again. Eventually my friend and his boss, who was the president of the company, met me for dinner one evening to discuss this further. They made me a nice offer, which after a few days' consideration, I accepted.

The company's name is VAM USA and its line of premium oilfield threads represents about half of the world's market. Most of the designs are of the coupled style and find use in many international oilfields. While they had a large presence internationally, they did not have a big market share domestically at that time. They did not have a good integral connection for long strings of pipe, called liners, until about six months before I joined the company. The tensile ratings on such a connection are enhanced by first expanding the box end of the connection and shrinking the pin end. This is done mechanically by a large press at room temperature. The ends of the pipe are next heated to a tempering temperature to remove the process stresses and then are air-cooled. The pipe is then threaded. The connection is called a semi-flush or expanded box connection because the OD is a little larger than the pipe. There is a need for this type of joint in the United States because companies are able to drill slimmer wells, thus saving money in rig time, mud, and other items. VAM USA focused on large oil companies who required lots of testing and technical support. Since most of the wells drilled in the U.S. are drilled by independents, the VAM line of connections was not a big factor at that time.

Promotional Tools

After a period of study I was assigned a number of accounts and was also given several projects. I had complained that our web site was not user-friendly and the president overheard my comments. He merely said, "You're right. Fix it!" I sent an email to a number of influential customers and asked them what information they would like on our site. I incorporated their thoughts and got with the consultant who had initially designed it. The only comment from my boss was to make sure that it still loaded quickly, staying under five seconds. After we made the changes, I emailed a large number of clients announcing our new site and asking them to click on it. I then monitored the number of hits to the site. I was astounded to see that the traffic tripled within days. Over the years I assisted in adding pages of supplementary information to the site.

I've had a lot of fun when meeting with new accounts and trying to encourage them to make use of this tool. If they seem reluctant to do so, I'll tell them it'll load in five seconds or I'll buy their lunch at any Burger King in the area. That usually breaks down their reluctance and we then get in the site and I show them some things that can help them. Because I've used this tool so often, I've had situations where that familiarization helped me walk them through it even when I wasn't in front of a computer. Our web site has been instrumental in reducing incoming calls about trivial matters, in making our products easier to use, and has increased our customer base.

The company had a sixty-page bound catalog that showed the features of the connections as well as a lot of dimensional and other information. However, I noticed that our competitors relied on self-standing ring binders with their company name prominently displayed on the spine instead of catalogs. Our literature either ended up sandwiched between these more visible items in the client's book case or laying flat in their desk drawer. We had a few customized ring binders out there but most were the result of a group presentation to the client and a number were very old. After discussing this internally, we decided to issue a standardized ring binder that included sections for our catalog, lists of distributors, accessory threaders, sales and service contacts, and end-users, as well as additional technical information. Our company's name is on the spine of these books and serves as an inexpensive 24/7 advertisement. When the company replaced our large technical catalog with a number of four-page color-coordinated flyers for different products, the ring binder became a convenient place for our clients to place them. As I handed them the new literature I offered to recycle the old catalog—as well as any of our competitors' booklets they wanted to get rid of. That always produced a laugh.

We have advertised in local technical society newsletters and have found it to be an efficient vehicle to reach a very targeted audience. A representative from the sales function is usually included in the early stages of a new ad campaign and that input can be helpful in expressing features in appropriate ways.

One day shortly after I joined the company, I walked into our local community college, located two miles from our office, to inquire about their racquetball program. While there I happened to see our neighbor who was an adjunct professor with the college. We talked briefly and she asked if the company I was with needed any sort of technical training. I told her that our computer skills were not very good and there was lots of room for improvement. I later introduced her to our management and before too long we were all attending classes on Microsoft Outlook, Excel, and Word.

A friend of mine gave an informal talk to a group of

us on "The Seven Habits of Highly Effective People." I mentioned that to the president of our company and he became interested. My friend was licensed to give such talks to clients. I introduced them and before too long my friend was contracted to conduct sessions on this to the sales and management personnel of the company.

Being Bold

I was asked to look at what we needed to do to enhance the introduction of our new semi-flush connection, VAM SLIJ II. We had literature on it but that was about it. I gathered as much running history information as I could as well as summaries of a number of test reports we'd done to qualify the connection. I presented this data to my customers but initially could not get any interest generated. Part of the problem was a well-entrenched competitor whose connection was similar in ratings.

An opportunity presented itself when a guru at one of the major oil companies sent out an email to us and three of our competitors with the names of all of us in the "To:" field. It said that they were soliciting bids for a new project and, in addition to the quote, would like each company to submit a plan to qualify their semi-flush connection in accordance with a rather involved test. In a bit of humor at the bottom of the email he said, "Hint, do not hit 'Reply to All.'"

We debated long and hard about the best way to present our test proposal. One strategy was to have the end-user pay for the $110,000 cost of the test. Typically, however, that would not be accepted by the end-user, especially if a competitor agreed to do it for free. Another scheme was for us to pick up that cost but to propose a higher price per connection for the project's duration until the cost of the test was satisfied. After much haggling internally, we got our management to agree that we would pay for half of the test and would not raise the price of the connections to pay for it. In addition, we said that if we did not successfully pass the test our customer would not owe us anything. Our gamble paid off. Two of our competitors declined to bid and the other one's bid was not accepted. We passed the test and were given a purchase order for the connections for that project.

That was a real feather in our cap and I started talking about it to engineers on other projects at that company. When one customer mentioned to me that he'd ordered our competitor's thread, I asked why. He indicated that he thought it was a better connection. I disagreed with that assessment and he said, "Okay, prove it." He produced the competitor's catalog and asked what my tension rating was on a certain size, weight, and grade of pipe. It turned out that our rating was better. He then asked what our compressive rating was and I showed him that ours was higher. He then suggested we compare ODs, because he figured our joint was not as slim. Again we were better. He then said, "You were better on that particular size, weight, and grade of pipe, let's try another one." The pipe gods were with me that day as ours was better in all three categories. He picked another one and we beat it again. He then said, "Ah, but I'll bet yours is more expensive." I said I didn't think so and suggested he ask for a formal quote. We eventually got his business.

I was so pleased with that process that I began to ask engineers on other projects what pipe they were using and told them I'd do ratings comparisons for them on the connections. I'd send them the results and then follow-up with another meeting to see what they thought of the results. I put so many of these comparisons together that my company requested that I put a composite one together for all of our technical personnel to use. Out of nearly twenty sizes and weights of connections, comparing tension, compression, and OD (sixty data points), there were only four entries in which the competitor's design was better and two in which it was a tie. This became a useful tool in increasing our exposure and therefore our business volume.

One large oil company had a platform that had many wells on it. One of our competitors had been given the order for their threads to be used on the completions before I had been assigned this account. The material coordinator for that project preferred our competitor's products and did not want to change. Even though we had passed the test as described above, and I could demonstrate that our connection was superior and had a better price, that didn't seem to matter to him. When I discussed this with the engineers in that group, they said the material coordinator always told them that the competitor's thread was bought through their primary distributor with cancelable and returnable terms. What he didn't tell them was that our threads could also be bought through that same distributor under the same exact terms. I debated confronting him but did not want to make him mad. About this time my boss got the distributor to sign a letter saying that our threads could be obtained under cancelable and returnable terms. From that time forward, whenever an engineer raised the objection they had been given by the material coordinator, I'd show him that letter. Over his protests, we eventually got all the subsequent work on that platform.

That major oil company became my best account as well as our company's biggest one. I had contact names of over 200 individuals at that one account and made it a point to position myself as a consultant to them. They gave me a security badge that allowed me to get into almost every floor on their four building campus.

Marketing to Small Firms

The domestic oil industry is very different than the international one in that there are many more independent oil companies. They are experts at finding and producing their crude or natural gas but they do not refine these products nor sell them directly to consumers. However, integrated oil companies do have those additional capabilities and include owning and franchising filling stations. A few independents have more drilling rigs working for them than any of the major integrated oil companies. Selling products into this market is very different than selling to a major oil company. The independents don't typically require a lot of demonstration testing since they figure the major oil companies have already taken care of that requirement. They are more interested in low price, fast delivery, and favorable terms. In addition, they are not in a position to place an order for a platform quantity of pipe but may only require one or two strings a year. Our brand name was not strong in this market segment because the company had not spent a lot of time cultivating it. Many of the smaller companies in places like Oklahoma City, Tulsa, Denver, and Dallas were unfamiliar with our company and its products. We found that persistence in making trips to these areas and participating in fundraiser barbecues, professional society meetings, industry golf tournaments, etc., earned us the right to be heard. People seemed to appreciate the effort we were making.

The novelty of having a salesperson call a contact in a remote city can be useful in setting up an initial call. I make it a point to use words like "brief visit" and "what we are doing for others" when setting up that first appointment. This lets the customer know that I am not asking for a large time commitment and that I plan on sharing some valuable information that has been useful to others and therefore might help him. A few contacts won't respond to phone calls and I've seen situations where a cold call works better. Even dropping off a business card to a receptionist for later follow-up can be useful. I've been able to reach an otherwise hard-to-reach contact by calling from the house phone in the company's lobby. The person I was calling thought it was the receptionist calling him. It is imperative to get the customer's business card on that first call. It is invaluable for later communications because it typically gives an email address and various phone numbers.

In setting up appointments for the week, I typically rank who I need to see based upon their importance to what I am trying to accomplish. For instance, if there is a big quote to be delivered, I might want to see the account one more time before it is sent out. Or, if there is a problem we are trying to solve for a given customer, I might need to see him as soon as possible. I usually send out an email asking when the next available time might be or when would be a good time for a business lunch. I try not to suggest a specific time initially since I am sending out multiple emails and want to avoid schedule conflicts. Once I set up the time, I sometimes email the contact with a suggested agenda and ask if there is anything else he'd like to suggest we talk about.

Computer Use

I've found the use of emails in setting up sales calls to contacts in other cities to be especially efficient. About ten days before a planned trip, I send out emails to a number of individuals telling them I'm contemplating a trip to their city and asking what days they might be available. If I don't get enough responses to justify the trip, it is easy to postpone it for another time. This technique saves money on long distance phone calls and prevents me from spending a lot of time on the phone.

I am especially aware of typos in emails. Poor spelling, bad grammar, and making errors like using "to" when "too" is meant, show a lack of professionalism. All word processing and email programs have spell check programs and can suggest alternate ways of saying things. I have the computer automatically check my spelling before any email is sent and I proof it several times to catch instances of poor word usage.

Email can be a great tool but can cause problems if care isn't taken in its use. For instance, the legal department of a major oil company handed one of its engineers a stack of emails he had sent over a several year period. The company was being hammered in the press because of a series of environmental and safety incidents and he was pleased that he'd thought to write all his prior correspondence in a professional and discreet way. One of his co-workers, however, had said things in a flippant and easily misunderstood way and was put in the embarrassing position of having to explain his terminology.

I rarely use the "Bcc:" field in sending out emails. I had a bad experience once when the person to whom I'd copied as a blind recipient responded to me and the other people on the distribution. It was obvious to the other addressees that I did not want them to see that another was copied on the email without their knowledge. If it is necessary for another to see an email, I forward it to him.

The computer can also be a valuable resource in staying up to date with the latest information in a given industry. I've utilized "Google Alerts" to learn more about certain companies and have been able to tell my customers more about their company than they know. This impresses them that I care enough about them and their firm that I would go to that trouble. The internet can also be used to see what is being said about competitors, mergers and acquisitions, new product introductions, and even your own company. I've found that annual reports can be another good source of information about my client's plans.

Presentations

VAM USA is a big believer in presentations to a number of personnel from the same company. These group discussions have been a useful tool in showing customers what we can do to help them. I typically meet with the client's contact person beforehand and ask him what issues he'd like addressed. I gather the persons who can best answer their questions and mobilize samples, flyers, and whatever else would be appropriate.

I've learned from experience to arrive at the client's location at least an hour before the presentation. This allows lots of time to handle any last minute problems like the bulb being burned out on the projector or someone neglecting to reserve a conference room.

If the group being addressed includes professional engineers or anyone whose credentials are dependent upon continuing education units (CEUs), I normally ask in the beginning of a talk if they'd like me to send them a letter verifying that they were in attendance. This is highly appreciated by anyone needing CEUs, sets us apart as being unique, and illustrates that the material to be presented is valuable.

I've found it useful to insert humor in talks and, if there are two people giving the talk, to alternate them as it helps the audience stay engaged. In one presentation, I told the group that my end-of-the year bonus depended upon them asking at least a dozen questions and asked them to help me reach that goal. I had some throw down questions prepared beforehand and got the ball rolling by looking at one individual and saying, "I'll bet you want to ask me about capacity, don't you?" I then encouraged him to ask that question and then proceeded to address it. I then said, "That's one." Humor (and the fear that they might be called upon to ask a question) kept them alert—and awake—during a 1½ hour talk that could have been a very boring exercise. Having them pass around samples of hardware, in our case 4½" anodized aluminum threaded parts, is also useful to demonstrate the product's features and encourages questions.

To overcome the fear of getting in front of an audience, I suggest getting involved with Toastmasters International or volunteer to speak in front of friendly audiences at church or community functions. I have given over 500 speeches to a variety of groups in both business and volunteer functions and it has served to make me more comfortable in these situations.

One large oil company wanted every service company involved in two of their big projects to attend a weekly meeting to discuss progress on the projects. They found this to be a good way to get all the various groups talking to each other and to advise the oil company of any upcoming schedule delays or issues. I found these meetings helpful and they also served as a vehicle for me to visit my customers on a regular basis. It had the effect of making all the participants feel like they were a part of a team and to pull together for the common good of the project. However, over a period of time, the meetings became routine and boring. Everything went well and we ran out of things to talk about. One of the young engineers at the oil company suggested that we have one supplier at each meeting make a presentation to the group about his product.

I knew that a detailed talk by each service company would probably be boring to the other vendors and my product especially so. I like to tell people we machine the ends of a piece of pipe to expose the VAM thread that was there all along. I figured that the first one of these talks would be well attended by my contacts at the oil company and by the other vendors, and whoever gave the first talk would set the standard. So, I was the first to volunteer to give a forty-five minute talk.

Before I left the office, I grabbed some sports bags left over from a prior event we had sponsored for our customers. When I got up in front of the group I told them that my talk was really going to be a test to see how much they knew about my company and our products. My first question was, "Who knows what VAM stands for?" (That is always a sucker question because the company is 51% owned by an international steel firm named V&M.). Of course several people hollered out "V and M." "No, you're wrong," I said. There was silence and one of the senior engineers, who had remembered this from a prior conversation, quietly mumbled that he thought the "V" stood for a steel company named Vallourec (which is the "V" in "V&M") and the last two initials had to do with the engineer's name who designed the first VAM thread. I said, "Close enough," and pulled out a sports bag and gave it to him. The group laughed about the unconventional turn that the presentation was taking and realized this was going to be a fun learning experience.

I then related how Alexandre Madrell was in charge of an engineering group in the early 1960s and was assigned the task of designing a metal-to-metal seal connection on oilfield pipe. From there I explained the evolution of the technology and why we have so many different designs of connections. I asked them other questions and handed out additional sports bags as we later discussed other facets of our company's products, services, and operations. I received a hearty round of applause at the end of the talk and a "thank you" from some of my oil company contacts. A couple of my peers at other service companies feigned disapproval as I had set the standard for subsequent talks they had to give.

At VAM USA, we set goals in the beginning of the year concerning how many talks like this will be given throughout the year. We also line out how many will include our engineering personnel or employees from other divisions. This information, as well as the number of sales calls made on end-user and distributor personnel, industry events attended, etc., is reported monthly as a part of the company's total quality management program (TQM).

Being Unique

There is something to be said about being different from the rest of the technical personnel calling on my customers. I am constantly trying to find ways to differentiate the products I promote, so why not myself? I've asked a number of clients what they look for in a good sales engineer. The most common responses I get include product knowledge and availability. We are a resource to them so it is incumbent upon us that we either help them with the requisite information or know where to get it. A quick response to any request for data or a call to them explaining that we are trying to get the information is always appreciated.

Having said all that, there are a number of things I've found that can distinguish me from my competitors. When visiting an important client, especially for the first time, I usually follow-up with a handwritten note thanking him for his time and looking forward to working with him in the future.

During the course of building rapport with a client, I try to determine what interests we have in common as I ask him leading questions about himself, what he enjoys, his family situation, sports participation (both now and when he was in school), or other activities in which he is currently involved. People enjoy doing business with someone who is like them and I therefore highlight those aspects of our lives that we have in common. At the end of a first call on a new customer, I usually ask him what his outdoor sport of choice is. That is something that clients have not been asked before and that usually gets a chuckle along with some information for later use. I then store this in my contacts file. Interjecting some aspect of a person's personal life in a subsequent conversation is a great way of strengthening relationships and expressing uniqueness because I remembered something about him.

When visiting with a customer and his phone rings, I encourage him to answer it. I'm not convinced that most salesmen do that. I do it because I want his attention and therefore I'd rather him handle the phone call so we can resume the conversation uninterrupted. While he's talking, I use the time to update my notes and look around his office for important clues about him, his interests or business. It also allows me the opportunity to gather my thoughts, organize literature to give him, and determine my next step.

I've made it a point to buy stock in my customers' companies. This allows me to demonstrate that I have some "skin in the game" and thus have their best interests at heart. I've found it easy to carry on conversations with them about the current and historical stock price, the price earnings (PE) ratio and other issues. By buying even just a single share, I automatically receive their annual report. Besides containing financial information, it typically includes a description of the company's success and its long term plans.

I've discovered that special events help distinguish me from my competitors. With certain large accounts, I occasionally organize a customer appreciation lunch at a local restaurant. I also invite my company's upper management to attend and meet them. This is always well received and allows interaction about issues of concern to both. It is especially gratifying when my clients realize that I know more of their fellow employees across their various business units than they do. When we are awarded with an especially large and important order I make it a point to celebrate the occasion with my client and any distributor involved with the sale. We may go to a dinner, baseball game, or even a play. This also is a good occasion to informally go over any outstanding issues and helps solidify the order.

There are a number of things about any company with whom I am employed that I cannot control. On-time delivery, quality, product offerings, etc., are elements outside of my responsibility. However, I can make sure I am always on time for appointments, that I do what I have committed to do, and am responsive to my customers' needs. This level of service is appreciated by clients and is a valuable and unique asset to an employer.

Summary

VAM USA has sent me to technical symposiums, as well as sales and sales management seminars. I've attended day long classes on various computer programs. I've become more aware of the importance of the relational aspect of the oil industry and have been challenged to learn the needs of both large and small companies. I've seen the advantage in taking bold steps and trying to be unique and I've learned the effectiveness in delivering entertaining but informative presentations.

As VAM USA has grown substantially over the years the need for clear communications between the various departments and management has increased. Sales personnel typically do not enjoy doing forecasts, monthly reports, trip reports, and the myriad of other documents that may be required. In some ways a sales engineer must function as a reporter, giving accurate information on the state of the industry and the need for new products. Maintaining a log book of various discussions with customers, distributors, and other employees makes it easier to accomplish this. When people see me writing down what they are saying, it makes them more thoughtful in their responses and raises the level of the discourse.

In a lot of ways, working for a manufacturing and service company forces the sales engineer to function as an orchestra conductor. He may call upon personnel in engineering, transportation, inside sales, accounting, manufacturing, and the service department to insure that a given project goes smoothly. It is his responsibility to use all the available resources of the company to keep his customers satisfied so they'll continue to buy from his firm. Instead of pointing a baton at the various players, he uses verbal communication, humor, emails, and a respectful and grateful manner in making a beautiful melody.

8
Other Things I've Learned

In business, honesty is absolutely essential. The best principle is "under promise and over deliver."

—Richard Denny, sales trainer

During the course of my ongoing career I've learned a number of sales principles that have helped me in most of the various positions I've held.

The Sales Engineer's Role

Unlike someone who is providing a one-time or occasional purchase of a product or service like a car, life insurance, a home mortgage, or an appliance, the sales engineer's effectiveness depends upon establishing long-term relationships. He may be involved in a project long before it is sanctioned as the customer tries to ascertain what he needs and how much it might cost. He helps ensure that once the order is placed that all the involvement his company might have with this order are correctly communicated and completed. He is there to work out problems and make sure the project moves along smoothly.

He asks if there are other items that the customer needs or wants. In many industries, there is usually a need for a field service representative to help install or commission the equipment. There may be issues involved with interfacing my equipment with that of a supplier of complementary equipment. There are technical issues that arise from time to time that the sales engineer has to make sure are properly addressed. Some clients expect a representative of the manufacturer to attend meetings on a periodic basis along with other suppliers to discuss schedules, equipment interfaces, field support, and address other issues that no one had previously considered. These tasks usually fall to the sales engineer since he is closest to the action, is expected to know what the client wants, and—because of long-term relationships—best knows the people involved.

Selling Techniques

The term "selling techniques" seems mercenary and evokes thoughts of being tricked into a sale. By virtue of the long-term relationships required by his discipline, a sales engineer would not last long using trickery or deceit in making a sale. Having said that, there are certain things a sales engineer can do in the process of getting in to see the customer, helping him determine what he needs, and supporting him afterwards. I have found that my customers are not offended when I tell them how I used a technique to help them and actually admire my passion, creativity, and persistence.

For instance, there is always the customer who will not return phone calls. Simply leaving a detailed message about what you want, why you need it, and that it is okay for them to say "no" to you will usually get a call back. Even if you don't have someone's email address, you can usually determine it by looking at his fellow employees' business cards.

When making that first contact with an account, it is helpful to start as high up in the organization as you can. That can feel intimidating. However, you might ask around to find who knows that high level person. I've made it a point to meet speakers at industry events and ask them who I should call on within their companies. You can gain an audience much easier with the lower level decision makers if you mention that so-and-so suggested you contact them.

I once had a customer whom I had called on for six years without selling his company anything. I knew they used my competitor's products but would not switch even though they knew mine were superior. At one point because I had nothing to lose, I decided to employ a technique suggested by Sandler. During separate conversations with three reps from this client, I said, "You know, it seems like your company will never use our products." There is something about the word "never" that makes a person want to correct you about the assumption you have made. In each case I got a response. I was able to determine that our competitor was pricing his products artificially lower than ours to maintain the business and that the client did not want to switch because of existing inventory of that product. I might not have discovered these issues had I not used that technique.

As someone involved in solving technical problems, I have tried hard to resist the temptation to immediately tell a customer I can solve his problem. When I visit a doctor he asks me lots of questions about what is ailing me in order to correctly diagnose the problem and suggest a cure. I question a doctor's judgment and the value of his advice if he immediately prescribes a solution without hearing all the facts. I've learned to ask lots of questions and then, if I think I have a solution, I tell the customer that we *might* have an answer and that I'll get back to him. I use that time to confer with technical resources to confirm that we can help and possibly uncover better solutions. This process sets us apart from 90% of the other sales reps out there and helps the customer realize that our advice is valuable.

I thought that the following quote from the U.S. Department of Labor (www.bls.gov/oco/ocos123.htm) was informative. "Sales Engineers tend to employ selling techniques that are different from those used by most other sales workers. They generally use a 'consultive' style: that is, they focus on the client's problem and show how it could be solved or mitigated with their product or service. This selling style differs from the 'benefits and features' method, whereby the salesperson describes the product and leaves the customer to decide how it would be useful."

Sales engineering is a consultive exercise in that the customer, in many cases, looks upon us as a part of the team. My customers know that I will tell them the truth because it is in my best interest to do so. If my product won't fit their current need, I tell them so because I know there will be other ones down the road that will. They also know that I have access to quality technical help at the home office.

I've discovered that just showing up can be a successful sales tool. Early in my career I had a customer who was very demanding and had intimidated other sales reps from my company when they had called on him. I respected the man, because of his longevity in the industry and sensed that part of his demeanor was an act. He saw sales reps on Wednesdays and it was not necessary to make prior appointments. Most of my competitors did not take advantage of his open invitation to visit with him. After calling on him nearly every Wednesday for about six months I started to make sales to him, to the amazement of my company. After about a year, he would actually suspect that I was seeing him that day because I knew of a particular project that was coming up. He'd then give me the details and we would quote it. A technical sales rep cannot hide behind his desk but has to be out seeing the people.

When I am in the offices of one of my large accounts, I allow lots of time between appointments. Depending upon the account, I can usually sit in the reception area and use the time to write up the notes from the just completed appointment. I can also say hello to any of the other contacts at that account as they pass through that area. Many times they will say something that will eventually lead to business, or even ask me to come to see them and that I was on their mind about something. I call this technique "lobby loitering."

Sales engineering is not an endeavor where one puts high pressure on a customer to buy his product. I find that simple statements at the end of a conversation like, "Hope we can work with you" are appropriate. I've closed opportunities, where I had previously laid the groundwork by asking lots of questions and providing answers, by merely inquiring of my customer, "What do you want me to do now?" If I hit a technical, commercial, or relational barrier with my client, I've learned to ask, "If you were me, what would you suggest I do?"

I've concluded that at times I must function as if I were docking a large ship. The line that ultimately secures the vessel to the dock is too heavy and stiff to throw to the men on the shore. So a boatswain's mate throws a heaving line with a lead weight enclosed in a "monkey fist." If necessary, a second line, called a messenger line, is attached to the end of the heaving line. To this is attached the "mooring line" or hawser. It takes time, patience, and persistence to be effective in individual sales opportunities and in this discipline, strengthening the lines of relationship one step at a time.

Entertainment

The purpose of entertaining customers is to enhance your company's business. In the sales engineering profession, it is rarely a quid pro quo situation as in, "If you take me to the ball game I'll buy from you." That is an unethical proposition and I'd run from it. Most of my clients only allow themselves to be entertained by companies with whom they are already doing business. This avoids any hint of impropriety. I usually discuss some item of business while I'm out with a customer, whether it is what their upcoming needs are, some new service we are offering, or some problem that needs to be addressed. It helps me to better understand an individual during conversations at lunch or watching how he plays golf. The value to my client's company is that, in effect, my customer is working extra hours for the benefit of his employer as he learns more of what we can do for him, whether it's more capacity, a new product, better delivery, etc. For both salesman and client, it promotes a friendly exchange of information in a non-threatening way.

Some companies ask their purchasing and engineering personnel to report when and with whom they've been entertained. I am cognizant of this and try not to ask any one person too often because I don't want him to feel compromised by going with me when he shouldn't or embarrassed because he has to say no. I occasionally bring pastry to my customers' offices if we've scheduled a morning meeting. On several occasions I'd asked one particular contact at a large oil company if he'd like me to bring donuts. He always refused and one day he asked that I not even offer to do that anymore. It turned out that his company's policy requires that he report any such offer, even something as inexpensive as pastry! There have been cases where clients take advantage of sales people and their desire to entertain them. In most instances it is obvious from their demeanor and the possible business to be gained that this is happening. I once asked a customer to lunch and when I picked him up he mentioned that the other guys (I thought, "What other guys?")

would meet us at the restaurant. Well, it turned out to be one of the most expensive establishments in town. After a costly meal including two bottles of wine with him and three of his fellow employees, I realized I could use this lunch as a way of getting a lot more information about their needs, schedules, etc., than I would have gotten otherwise. During the course of the meal, I humorously acknowledged that the bill was going to be a big one. I also mentioned that we were having a hard time getting information about their project. The remorse they felt about taking advantage of the situation caused them to email me all sorts of important information that eventually helped us. Guilt can be a very powerful force.

Over the years I've learned some interesting things while entertaining customers. A five-minute conversation with an industry guru on the back of a fishing boat explained where we stood on a very large project. A lunch with another individual helped clarify the best way to fashion a proposal to meet his company's needs and ultimately led to millions of dollars of business. A brief comment from another customer while playing a round of golf alerted us of some pending litigation. However, most occasions only resulted in our client knowing that we were committed enough to their business and confident about our ability to serve them that we were not afraid to spend money meeting with them. When I first became self-employed I gulped when I found myself in a situation being expected to pick up the lunch tab for six client personnel. My being willing to do so smoothed the discussions and resulted in a very nice sale. If baseball games, dinners, or plays involve spouses it is even better.

This type of entertainment can help solidify long-term relationships and is a way of thanking existing customers for their business.

Another form of this involves a group of client personnel being entertained and educated at the same time. I have participated in plant tours, "lunch and learns," chili cook-offs, and customer receptions. At company sponsored golf tournaments I've placed a sign on each of twenty-seven tee boxes mentioning some factoid about our company. Standing there, waiting to tee off, my customers couldn't help but learn some new thing about our company. Industry-wide and professional society events offer a non-threatening way to visit a lot of client personnel. Nearly all business segments have annual golf tournaments, charity cooking events, fishing tournaments, and the like. I've found that attendance at trade shows, even at those for which my company does not have a booth, is a good way of visiting with clients.

Planning and executing these events requires a lot of detail work and can be time consuming. At times I've felt like a social director on a cruise ship. However, it pays off in the long run as I learn more about my customers, their needs and personalities.

When A Mistake is Made

There are times when companies with whom I have been associated made a mistake. It usually has to do with a delivery, quality control, or communication problem. In these cases, it is left to the sales engineer to meet with the customer and resolve the issue. In these situations, I first admit the mistake and then apologize for the inconvenience we have caused the customer. This is something that can cause a sales engineer to be viewed as unique because no one wants to apologize, especially for something he personally did not do.

I was visiting with a client once who was irritated that he was continually having transportation issues with my company. He complained about trucks waiting too long for load outs. While I was in his office, my counterpart at a competitor's company called him and he began to chew him out for the same thing. After he hung up he grinned at me sheepishly and said, "All you guys have the same problem." Well, I apologized for us having this issue and went back to my company's plant to alert them to the problem and see what we could do to fix it. I thought it had been resolved only to find out six months later that the same issue surfaced again. I was getting tired of apologizing and brought the head of our shipping department to meet with my customer. I introduced them to each other and suddenly it was as if I was not in the room. They started sharing the common problems they were having with truckers, finding good help, and other issues. They discussed some ways to avoid delays in the future and the problem rarely surfaced again.

On another occasion, a manufacturer I represented shipped some conveyors to a client on some large wooden pallets. The legs of the conveyors were not secured on top of the two-by-four runners but instead rested on the one-inch thick planks of the pallets. During transit across the country, this caused the legs to become damaged. I could clearly see what the issue was and immediately apologized to the client. I took pictures to show the manufacturer, who then replaced the legs free of charge.

I was once asked to provide a magnetic trap for a rice company to remove tramp metal from the flow of rice before it went through a bag packer. It consisted of a custom designed stainless steel housing in which a grate of rare earth magnets was placed so the rice would flow through it. Unfortunately, when I provided the measurements to the manufacturer, I didn't take into account the thickness of the metal housing. As a consequence, it didn't fit properly. It was my fault, so I apologized to the customer and the manufacturer and we had to build another one. I didn't make much money on that sale but I also didn't make that mistake again.

A friend of mine with a downhole tool company had the unenviable task of apologizing and explaining to his customer how it was the malfunction of a certain piece of equipment cost the customer about a million dollars extra during the completion of an oil well. Fortunately, he had gone to college with the oil company's manager who suggested that whatever he did to rectify the situation, he should make it a win-win for both companies. My friend proposed that if they would commit to buy products at a certain level from his company for the following two years, they would provide discounts equaling two million dollars. That's called making lemonade out of lemons!

Some of these situations can be highly charged emotionally. In these cases I pretend I am a robot whose purpose is to find out what the problem is. The procedure I follow is to first let the customer vent his frustration. I then ask as many questions as needed to get to the bottom of what happened. I express sorrow for causing a problem and explore some possible solutions by asking the customer what he thinks would make it right. Without committing to a solution, I tell the client I will get back to him promptly once I concur with my management. This method usually disarms the situation and allows time to come up with a satisfactory solution. By taking my emotions out of it I avoid being defensive or saying something I will later regret.

Negotiating

There are times when I have had to negotiate with a client in order to get his business. In many cases, it is an issue of price to the customer. However, I've learned that once I provide a quote I should not just unilaterally lower the price when the customer complains. That is a sure way to lose respect from the customer, set a bad precedent, and hurt future sales.

I once was quoted a per day rental rate for a car in another city. I decided to check with another company and got offered a lower rate. I called back the first company, gave them the price the other guys quoted and they immediately matched it. Instead of making me happy, it made me mad that I had to go to all that trouble to get a comparative rate when I had assumed through all my years of dealing with the first company that they had always given me a fair rate. I don't use them anymore.

When a customer tells me that my price is too high, I try to determine how much higher it is. I then discuss this with my management and marketing personnel to fashion an appropriate response. The answer, depending upon the numbers involved, might be to do nothing. We may not be able to meet the price. However, in many cases, we have found ways to counter with something we want that might not mean much to the customer. For instance, we might propose a lower price now in exchange for his increasing the size of the order, committing to a long-term agreement, allowing us more flexibility on timing, buying ancillary items from us, giving us periodic information on their needs, paying promptly, agreeing to an exclusive contract, or other items that might not mean that much to the client but do to us. This sort of quid pro quo maintains the customer's respect for our company and is a win for both sides. Sometimes a sales engineer must function as a diplomat and allow both sides to save face and gain an advantage.

When You Lose a Sale

I've always found it a little heart wrenching when I lose a sale. My company has spent time putting a quote together, and I've invested emotional and intellectual energy in the proposal and maybe even foolishly told management that it's a done deal. And then the phone rings and the customer let's me know it's someone else's done deal.

Because we are professionals and we are always doing our best to please our customers, our first reaction is to stoically tell the customer, "Thanks anyway, I understand." However, I've learned that the customers respect you more if you hesitate a little and carefully allow some disappointment to show through. After all, we've provided a service to them by allowing them to look at our quote and learn what other products and services are available. Our company has spent some effort in getting them the information to make an intelligent decision. We are people, too, and expect something in return, even if we don't get that sale.

Because the purchaser may feel a little guilty about having to give me the bad news, now is the time to ask some questions.

"Who got the order?"

"Was it price?"

"If so, by how much did we miss it?"

"Was there a technical or delivery issue in play?"

These are just a few of the questions we should be prepared to ask. It is to the advantage of the purchaser to tell you as much as possible so you can be ready for the next opportunity. At least I can cut my losses somewhat by getting some valuable information. I always leave the door open by telling them if something changes or the existing supplier can't meet his needs we are there to help. I want to make it easy for my customer to give me another shot in the future.

9
Sales Engineering: A Wonderful Profession

If you work just for money, you'll never make it. But if you love what you are doing, and always put the customer first, success will be yours.
> —Ray Kroc, co-founder of McDonald's

A young technical sales representative mentioned to me once that she couldn't believe that her company actually pays her to entertain customers by taking them to play golf, go out to eat, attend functions, etc. She said technical sales must be a well-kept secret.

It's not so much a secret as the fact that this profession is not for everyone. The sales engineer has to understand technical issues and terms. In addition he (or she) has to deal with real or perceived rejection, customer attitudes, company mistakes, and lack of structure. He has to be able to give presentations and be enthused about the products or services he is representing. Sometimes management is not supportive. I've been in situations where the boss groused that the sales guys are never around and also in those where management complained that the sales guys should not be around!

During my manufacturer's rep days I called on an engineer whose office was deep in the bowels of a chemical plant. You could tell that the headquarters building in which he sat was old but at one time had been a magnificent edifice. His office was very large and I commented on that. I also asked him how long he had worked for the company. He told me he had been there twenty-two years and he had always sat in that room. At one time it had held four people and as the company went through various changes and downsizings he moved from one corner of the room to the other as his associates moved on. I thought that that was one of the most depressing environments in which to work and I was glad my position afforded more mobility.

I've often asked myself what it is about this profession that I find so compelling. I think there are a number of things including freedom, the challenge of managing an account, the satisfaction of enlisting the right resources to solve a problem, and the euphoria of making a sale, to name a few. The business contacts a professional salesman makes become a personal asset of his that he can take along with him to other opportunities.

There is a move by consumers to buy products, especially electronic equipment, on the internet. There have been attempts to sell industrial equipment using this medium. Some have even tried conducting reverse auctions, in which manufacturers compete against one another via the internet. To my knowledge, neither has been successful with industrial equipment. It is very hard to commoditize technical products and to quantify the difference in quality and value among suppliers. These attempts are analogous to the automated telephone response systems where you press "1" for yes and "2" for no.

The products and services that a sales engineer represents are technical and require him to function, at various times during the sales process, as a teacher, doctor, diplomat, scout, etc. Suppliers who retain sales engineers can be more competitive than those who don't because people like to deal with other people in this increasingly complex selling environment. Computers can't do relational selling. There will always be a need for friendly people who can explain difficult things in an easily understood way. For these reasons, I feel that the demand for sales engineers will continue to grow.

It is challenging to learn the features of a new product or service and what it can do for your customer. I count it as a blessing that circumstances have forced me to be involved in a number of different industries and market segments. The common thread throughout my career is the pleasure derived from serving my customers by helping them get what they need. Bring on the next sales opportunity!

Topical Index

What you can do when:

a mistake is made 131–134

addressing the customer's problem 19

leaving a message 66

making that first contct 125

planning your week 16, 74, 111

sending emails 112–113

setting up sales calls in other cities 112

the customer says your price is too high 134–135

the customer won't pay 51–55

the industry changes 27, 35, 40

the sales call is interrupted 118

they won't call back 66, 125

you lose a sale 135–136

you first start out.. 15–16

you need email addresses 111, 125

Why it's important to:

be a professional engineer..22

entertain your customers 128–131

get business cards 111

know your territory 16–17

know your customer's personality...................... 20–21

see customers 127

sell solutions, not products.................................. 19, 85

How technical selling is like being a:

Boatswain's Mate 128

Doctor 55, 101, 126

Diplomat.. 135

Farmer... 59, 75

Orchestra Conductor.. 120

Reporter 120

Robot 133

Scout..81, 83, 85

Social Director... 131

Teacher..30